A YEAR OF
LIVING THANKFULLY

A YEAR OF LIVING THANKFULLY

A WEEK-BY-WEEK WORKBOOK TO HELP YOU EMBRACE GRATITUDE AND DISCOVER A HEALTHIER, HAPPIER YOU

LOIS BLYTH

CICO BOOKS
LONDON NEW YORK

Published in 2019 by CICO Books
An imprint of Ryland Peters & Small Ltd
20–21 Jockey's Fields, London WC1R 4BW
341 E 116th St, New York, NY 10029

www.rylandpeters.com

10 9 8 7 6 5 4 3 2 1

Text © Lois Blyth 2019
Design and illustration © CICO Books 2019

Adapted from *The Power of Gratitude,*
also published by CICO Books.

A CIP catalog record for this book is available from the Library of Congress
and the British Library.

ISBN: 978 1 78249 727 1

Printed in China

Editor: Dawn Bates
Designer: Alison Fenton
Illustrator: Daniel Haskett
In-house designer: Eliana Holder
Art director: Sally Powell
Production controller: Mai-Ling Collyer
Publishing manager: Penny Craig
Publisher: Cindy Richards

CONTENTS

INTRODUCTION

There is much more to gratitude than giving, receiving, and saying thank you. It is a subtly positive way to gradually transform not only your world, but also the world of those around you—and, beyond that, the world we all live in. Gratitude can make great things happen because it has the capacity to open our hearts and show us the art of possibility. Feeling thankful is not always easy, but it offers a pathway to acceptance, in all its forms.

Whole-hearted gratitude is an uplifting, expansive, and positive way of being that leads to appreciation and times of fun and laughter. Sharing, caring, and togetherness are some of the essentials of being human. Feeling thankful makes us want to give back—to those who have helped us, cared for us, who love us—or who quite simply make us happy.

The magic happens when thoughts of gratitude are transformed into positive action. They become a gift of wholehearted appreciation that expands with further giving. Each time one person expresses gratitude to another, the feeling of being appreciated encourages both people to be more generous-spirited to others—and so it goes on.

Whether expressed in the warmth of kindness or friendship, the simplicity of a few written lines or a phone call, or the capacity to offer comfort to someone in pain, or symbolized in the form of a gift, gratitude is always about connection. It offers thanks with an awareness that life is not about "me," but about "us," and that relating to others offers greater joy than focusing on ourselves alone.

Gratitude may also offer comfort during times of grief and challenge. When we feel thankful, our perception shifts and the world becomes a place of greater optimism and hope. In remembering to value others for who they are or for what they bring to our lives, we are more likely to overlook or forgive those things that make us feel less than appreciative.

Perhaps more than anything else, living life with gratitude can put us back in balance. It is a conscious pathway to fulfillment and contentment. Thinking of the bigger picture can be humbling. Taking time to recognize everything we can be thankful for offers relief from disenchantment and allows us the freedom to be ourselves.

"NOTHING IS MORE HONORABLE THAN
A GRATEFUL HEART."

Seneca (4 BCE–36 CE), Roman philosopher

HOW TO USE THIS BOOK

The introductory pages that follow explore some of the benefits of living with more gratitude, but also reflect on why it can be difficult sometimes. Then there is an activity for you to do each week of the year, including background information on how it can help you to be more thankful. If you miss a week, don't worry—this is meant to be fun, not a chore! Whatever works for you will be the right way to continue. There is no need to do the exercises sequentially. This is not a program—it is a creative place to explore your ideas and feelings. There are notes pages at the end of each week where you can record your thoughts and feelings about that particular activity and a checklist at the end of the book to help you to keep track. Maybe you can share some of the ideas with loved ones, too, and spread a little gratitude throughout the year! At the end of the book there is guidance on continuing your gratitude records with a journal.

The bigger picture

"I had become fed up with certain aspects of my job," says Grace, "and was thinking of leaving. I was having trouble thinking of anything positive to write in my gratitude journal, too, so I flicked back through it, partly for inspiration. I came across a couple of entries that described how grateful I felt to get the job in the first place! That helped me to think about the bigger picture and things I can do to bring about changes in my place of work instead, rather than leaving and causing upheaval."

Writing is not for me. What are the alternatives?

There are as many ways to express our thoughts of gratitude as there are ways to express ourselves: photography, music, painting, doodling, and the spoken word all have power. You may simply want to collect some symbols of gratitude: a pebble from a beach, a concert ticket, a greetings card, or a letter.

The benefit of recording something in a permanent form is that it increases in depth and momentum over time—and it is always there to refer to. However, the essence of gratitude is that it has the capacity to become a powerful force for change and optimism, whether it is expressed occasionally or every moment of every day.

GETTING STARTED

Saying "thank you" is a common courtesy in every language—we all use this expression of gratitude every day. It is more than a polite habit of speech. When we focus on increasing our level of appreciation, we bring greater joy and enrichment to our lives. The intention throughout this book is not to overwhelm you with things to do and rituals to keep to, but simply to invite you to dip in with an open mind to the possibilities that living with gratitude can offer.

START WHERE YOU ARE

Gratitude begins with a first step: giving thanks for big things, small things, and people who matter. As optimism grows, we develop confidence and an increased will to make a difference—and gradually we influence those around us, too. The more frequently we step away from complacency and choose to move toward gratitude, the greater the possibility of diminishing indifference in our own lives and in the world around us.

Gratitude is not a destination; it is a state of mind and being. You can quite simply start where you are, right now, with three simple questions:

* Who do I feel grateful to have in my life?
* What has already happened today that I can be thankful for?
* How shall I record this moment or show my appreciation?

Making a habit of answering these questions can quickly make your life happier and more contented. You will learn more about how to answer these questions in the pages that follow.

NURTURING GRATITUDE

From pagan times to the present day, the rhythm and language of the seasons have become embedded in our way of life. Spring, especially, is associated with new growth and new beginnings. It is the ideal time to clear your mind and consciously get rid of unhelpful attitudes that are no longer serving your needs, to make space for the new attitude in residence: Gratitude.

Gratitude, like all newly planted seeds, needs patience, warmth, and nurture to allow it to grow and to give it the space and time to shine. It may be sensitive in the early stages of growth and easily suffocated by darker feelings of bitterness, anger, resentment, and jealousy, which absorb too much energy. By staying attentive and weeding out unhelpful attitudes, you can allow gratitude and thankfulness to burgeon.

Companionship, friendship, shared laughter, and kindness help gratitude to develop unabated. Regular feeding with appreciation, understanding, and courtesy also works wonders. But beware of doubt, suspicion, and cynicism; they are common pests that undermine sincerity. The moment any kind of ulterior motive is suspected, genuine thankfulness falters and finds it harder to thrive. With regular nurture, gratitude will flower into optimism and positivity that sustain health and well-being for life.

WHY GIVING THANKS MATTERS

We all need gratitude. We need to receive it so that we feel appreciated, and we need to extend it to others and to the world we are part of, to stay connected and appreciative of what we have.

Material possessions do not necessarily make us feel happier. How can we be gratefully satisfied with what we already have if we are always looking for something newer or better? There can be a tendency to feel less contented the more we own—because the more we have, the more we want. Tuning in to gratitude helps us to stay grounded. It is not about accepting the status quo, but about regaining perspective and appreciating all that is good about where we are and what we have right now.

> "WHEN YOU RISE IN THE MORNING, GIVE THANKS FOR THE LIGHT, FOR YOUR LIFE, FOR YOUR STRENGTH. GIVE THANKS FOR YOUR FOOD AND FOR THE JOY OF LIVING. IF YOU SEE NO REASON TO GIVE THANKS, THE FAULT LIES IN YOURSELF."

Tecumseh (1768–1813), Shawnee Chief

True contentment

In her book *Fragile Mystics* (2015), Revd. Magdalen Smith introduces us to Rosie Pinto de Carvalho, who tells her: "I don't have everything I love, but I love everything I have." Rosie lives in a favela in one of the poorest areas of Rio de Janeiro, Brazil. What an inspiring attitude to life! In that single comment, Rosie reinforces awareness that there is very little connection between material possessions and contentment. The less we own, the more we appreciate and treasure what our belongings represent.

THE SIX As OF THANKFULNESS

- Choose your **Attitude**—Finding ways to develop a consciously positive outlook is an integral part of becoming "thank full."

- Increase **Awareness**—Tuning in to your environment and the events of each day increases consciousness.

- **Appreciate** the everyday—Finding joy in small things expands our appreciation of the bigger things, too.

- **Allocate** time—If you are writing a journal, it can be helpful to do it at the same time each day, so that you begin to remember automatically.

- Remain **Authentic**—Everyone has their own style of behavior and of expression. Stay true to yourself.

- **Acceptance**—The most important "A" of all. Gratitude is at its most powerful when you allow others to give, and can accept wholeheartedly.

CREATING A SACRED SPACE

You can start to put gratitude into action right now, simply with a positive approach and an open heart. However, living with gratitude may be more powerful if practical tweaks and changes are made to the home and work environment, too.

Is there an area in your home where you can feel at peace? For some it will be a whole room, for others it may be a particular chair, or a spot by a window or outside in the garden.

This can become a sacred space for contemplation. If you feel anxious about the sense of ritual involved, be reassured that there is no need for any kind of faith or conscious belief for this process to be helpful. Making space within your world for a positive nook that you automatically associate with feelings of wholehearted thanks can trigger wonderful feelings of peace and acceptance.

A sense of calm is essential for replenishing feelings of gratitude, especially after a taxing or tiring day. Creating an area for contemplation can help you to feel more connected, focused, and grounded. Just as you would clear your work surfaces before preparing to cook or create something, so too it makes sense to clear your mind before focusing on all there is to feel grateful for.

CREATING A GRATITUDE ALTAR

Altars have played an important part in rites and rituals of thanksgiving since prehistoric times, as well as being an anchor point for receiving the sacrament in Western religions. They cross cultures and are often mobile, too. Armies use the drum as an altar in the battlefield (and still hold drumhead services to this day), and spiritual leaders around the world carry simple symbols of prayer with them at all times, in case of need.

Just as we may light a candle in remembrance or as a sign of peace, or display objects on a desk or mantelpiece to remind us of important moments in our lives, so an altar provides a surface where we can focus our attention and change our thought processes for a moment.

Creating an altar is very personal. If you feel moved to make one in your home, think about whether you want it to be in a place that is light and bright in the morning; or cozy and softly lit for use in the evenings. Do you want to be able to hear sounds of birdsong outside your window, or do you want silence or music so that you can shut out the world? You may like to include:

- Candles—scented or unscented
- Flowers
- Natural elements, such as pebbles, shells, and/or leaves
- Symbols that have personal meaning for you, such as a ring, crystals, or a sacred object

Altars provide a focus for offering thanks for all that life provides. Put to one side any doubts and preconceptions you may have about whether this will work, and allow yourself the time to create a beautiful space that makes you want to give from your heart, and open yourself up to greater understanding. (Note: If the word "altar" has serious religious significance for you, and you feel uncomfortable with the secular use, think of it simply as a table or platform where you can focus your attention on the power of gratitude.)

There are no rules about how you should express or focus on giving thanks. This is your personal route to experiencing gratitude, and no one else's.

"IT IS NOT HAPPINESS THAT MAKES US GRATEFUL;
IT IS GRATEFULNESS THAT MAKES US HAPPY."

Brother David Steindl-Rast (1926–), Benedictine Monk

GRATITUDE IS GOOD FOR US

Scientific research is gradually building a body of evidence that supports what
we have always known instinctively—that gratitude is good for our health. It shows
up not only in the way we look after our physical fitness and nutritional health, but
also in our mental well-being and lifestyle choices. Gratitude helps us to
develop an optimistic outlook and plays an important role in how we feel
about our life, work, and purpose.

We experience the impact of gratitude not only directly, through the impact on our
health and well-being, but also indirectly, through the power of positive thinking and
feelings of self-worth. Feeling gratitude for our work and fully embracing the varied
roles we have in life help to generate a sense of completeness—and of thankfulness for
this life, right here, right now.

Health experts and researchers around the world are starting to pay greater attention to gratitude and its impact on our health, thought processes, and behavior. From the Greater Good Science Center in Berkeley, California, to the University of Birmingham, England (in association with the John Templeton Foundation), scientists are measuring and assessing what makes us grateful and what happens when we are grateful. Early indications are that it is good for the heart as well as the soul.

In 2015, the *Journal of Happiness Studies* (yes, there really is such a publication!) reported on a short-term study in the United States that compared the benefits to patients of keeping a) a gratitude journal; b) a kindness journal; and c) no journal over a period of 14 days, while they were waiting to be referred to a counselor. Interestingly, the only group that felt any benefit during such a short period of time was the one that focused on gratitude.

What does a grateful brain look like?

Researchers have found that when people express gratitude, their brains show increased levels of activity in the anterior cingulate cortex and the medial prefrontal cortex. Both areas are associated with the way we process emotions and express empathy, our bonds with others, and moral judgment.

A team at the University of Southern California is looking into the benefits gratitude has on health and well-being. They are discovering that our simple habit of saying "thank you" goes far beyond being a ritual social exchange. Gratitude in all forms makes us feel appreciated, which stimulates areas of the brain that are linked to empathy, moral judgment, and bonding. Dr. Glenn Fox, who is leading the study, says he designed the experiment to assess the commonalities between "small feelings of appreciation and large feelings of gratitude." His team is discovering that patterns of brain activity show gratitude to be "a complex social emotion that is really built around how others seek to benefit us." It plays an important role in our sense of who we are as human beings, how we relate to and care for one another, and our sense of social belonging.

Did you know?

The University of California, Berkeley, runs the grateful-sounding Greater Good Science Center, which funds research into the long-term benefits of gratitude. Scientists at the center have discovered that people who practice gratitude regularly have been found to:

- Develop stronger immune systems and lower blood pressure
- Experience higher levels of positive emotion
- Have an increased sense of joy, optimism, and happiness
- Be more likely to act with generosity and compassion
- Feel less lonely and isolated

Visit their website to find out more about the latest research in this area (see Further Resources, page 189).

WHEN GRATITUDE DOESN'T WORK

There is one negative trait that can become associated with the habit of gratitude: some people have the potential to develop a false sense of reality. This can take the form of an extreme and rather fatalistic belief that life is so positive that everything will be okay, whatever the evidence to the contrary. This can lead to problems such as ignoring bills, not going to the doctor, not acknowledging that something needs to be repaired. Gratitude does not absolve us from responsibility; it is more about achieving balance— appreciating that life is about giving and receiving rather than expecting and taking.

There are times, too, when we just don't want to take the trouble to feel consciously thankful—and moments when it can be incredibly irritating to be confronted with a "Pollyanna" approach to life. Full-on, upbeat optimism is not always appropriate, and a healthy dose of cynicism or humor can be equally beneficial.

According to Professor Julie Norem of Wellesley College in Massachusetts, a forced state of optimism and gratitude can make some people extremely anxious. She calls this "defensive pessimism." An over-emphasis on positive thinking can lead to a worrying sense of uncertainty because it creates a false sense of reality. This is where Authenticity comes in, from the six As of thankfulness on page 14. If you are having a rotten day, it is normal to feel low, and gratitude may not come naturally. Trying to force yourself to believe that something bad is actually good can be both unhealthy and distressing. There are times when patience is the key to gratitude, since the positive side of a situation may not be immediately apparent.

There is nothing wrong, then, with self-doubt or struggling to think positively. Plenty of people start from the premise that only by imagining the worst that can happen can they be reasonably sure that they will not be disappointed, whatever the outcome. Then they are grateful when they are proved right!

REMEMBER TO BE AUTHENTIC

> "THE HARDER WE TRY WITH THE CONSCIOUS WILL TO DO SOMETHING, THE LESS WE SHALL SUCCEED."

Aldous Huxley (1894–1963), writer and philosopher

Taking time to feel grateful

"I became very interested in practicing positivity in a conscious way after a particularly difficult time in my life," says Gina. "I have been told that I am a bit of an 'Eeyore' in my approach to things, and I worry a great deal. I wanted to see whether consciously changing my thoughts would make a permanent difference. However, after an enthusiastic beginning I found that I began to feel guilty if I did not feel grateful straight away. Many of the self-help books made me feel worse instead of better—as if I was doing something wrong. Living with gratitude is not a simple matter of saying that 'the world is alright' and then it shall be so. Some serious work has to be done along the way to consciously change one's thoughts and approach. These days I take my time to feel grateful. I aim to reframe things in a more positive light."

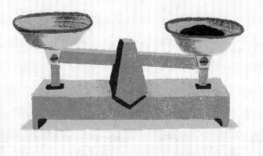

WHEN GRATITUDE IS DIFFICULT

Sometimes in life we are pitched a curveball. It can be hard to feel any sense of gratitude in the midst of a tragedy, illness, or disaster. But it is when we have the most to lose that we also have the most to gain. When life as we know it is torn away, we are left with a greater awareness of what is most important. This section takes a good look at how to cope when gratitude is difficult, and offers ways to reframe life's challenges with hope and forgiveness—and generosity.

WHY ME, WHY THIS, WHY NOW?

Gratitude does not come readily or immediately in every situation. It is highly unlikely, when a crisis strikes, that your first feelings will be of gratitude for the pain and suffering you are facing. A fractured leg? Thank you for the downtime! A broken heart? Great— I knew it was about time I experienced a period of loss and abandonment! Out of work? Bring it on—I am so pleased that I can no longer afford the payments on my house. A serious illness? Let's not even go there … no one would ever want to put their family or themselves through the trauma and fear of a life-threatening diagnosis.

And yet many people (although by no means all), after coming through a period of difficulty, will look back on their experience as a gift of some sort. The enforced period of recovery from accident or illness allowed time for reflection, or brought their family closer together; an unwanted redundancy led to a change of professional direction or a slimming-down of stressful financial commitments; a broken relationship is seen in hindsight from a healthier perspective—and the future represents something more positive. But while we are in the midst of disruption, gratitude can be elusive.

FEELING LOST

If you are in the middle of a dark forest and no one knows you are there, it is clear that there is little point in waiting to be found. You have to accept that you are lost. You may try to find your own way out, making determined efforts to keep warm, build a shelter, and avoid predators—but without experience, support, or knowledge of your terrain you may simply put yourself in greater danger.

Eventually, in order to get help, you create a din, clear a space, light a fire—do whatever is necessary to get yourself noticed, ideally without doing permanent damage or putting yourself in greater danger. In life, as in the forest, those who are in crisis may create a situation that requires the support of others—with luck, before it is too late for them to be saved.

To step toward gratitude we may first need to find the courage to face the reality of the present moment and ask for help. It is not only the person who feels lost who needs acceptance, but also those who offer love, support, or solace.

GRATEFUL ACCEPTANCE

How, then, can we learn to cope with our feelings when we are in the midst of trauma and distress? How can we find the will to play the long game and to look beyond the pain and discomfort of the present moment? The truth is that there is no easy answer. For some there will be the pathway to meditation or prayer, for others the comfort of friends and family—or the kindness of strangers. What is common to both routes, however, is taking a conscious decision to step away from our feelings of worry and isolation, or let go of the sense that we are alone with our fears and troubles, and try to look outward, to start reconnecting with the world around us.

In the words of the gratitude expert Robert Emmons, "Life is suffering. No amount of positive thinking exercises will change this truth." He acknowledges clearly through his research that forcibly adopting an artificially positive stance during times of trauma can have the opposite effect. "Keep calm and carry on" might be the only mantra you can manage at times of pressure.

TRANSFORMATION

Grateful acceptance is the state of fully absorbing the present state of affairs and seeking to discover what can be learned from it, what our role is within it, and how we can eventually feel grateful for the experience. There is no substitute for time and patience. It is through the cracks of life's darker and more challenging moments that we can see where the light shines most brightly.

We may be surprised to find that, following a period of distress and disturbance, our capacity for happiness and contentment gradually starts to increase. We start to focus on the good instead of the bad. We rediscover the joy in small things. Material things diminish in importance and we focus instead on the quality of our relationships. Most of all, we feel a sense of gratitude—for this, for here, for now.

"LIFE ISN'T ALL HA HA HEE HEE."

Meera Syal CBE (1961–), writer and actor

SOME GUIDANCE ON GIVING

When we give to others it's worth looking at our motives and thinking about how what we are offering—whether it's help or a gift—may be received.

RESPECTFUL GIVING

Have you ever had the experience of offering help to someone, only to have your offer refused? Those who are parents know only too well how that can feel. We all like to be appreciated, so when an offer of help is thrown back at us, it can feel like personal rejection. Before taking it personally, however, it can help to pause and think again—about how it may seem from the other person's point of view.

If life feels tough and you have been struggling in some way, the chances are that your sense of self has taken a battering, too. So when someone insists on giving you something that you do not feel you need, or that will make no tangible difference to the reality of your situation, it simply reinforces the lack that you already feel.

A person with a disability, who has learned to live independently, may rebuff a well-meaning arm to help them get on a train because they have had to cope unassisted for years; an elderly person who is feeling lonely may turn down a one-off invitation to lunch because coming home to an empty house reinforces the sense of aloneness; a homeless man who would love to eat turns down a tuna sandwich because, although he is hungry, he does not like tuna—and although he is in need, he is still able to exercise his right to choose.

Respect for others must be at the heart of any act of giving—and that means asking the person what kind of help they would like (if any). Giving without asking is not giving at all, it is about satisfying our own need to feel good about ourselves.

KEEPING THINGS SPECIAL

Children, especially, look forward each year to times of giving with enormous hope and excitement. Seeing a child's face as they receive and unwrap a gift is a precious treat in itself. But gifts lose their glister when we receive them too often. Expectations become greater and the magic of receiving diminishes, because it is no longer rare or special. It's the gift equivalent of your favorite song being played endlessly on the radio, or the festive lights losing their magic if they stay up after the party is over.

When anticipation is high and imagination vivid, a promising parcel can produce great expectations, and disappointment can follow hard on the heels of high hopes. So we learn early on that gifts are not necessarily all they seem: the simplest gift can be the most exciting, and the plainest parcel may contain a surprising and wonderful reward. With guidance, children learn not to expect, but to be open to receiving and always to appreciate, so that they are pleasantly surprised and rarely disappointed.

Who is giving to whom?

Gift-giving can become stressful when it becomes more about personal need than the wish to honor someone else. Perhaps...

- The giver becomes so concerned about causing disappointment that they can no longer trust their own judgment to choose
- In an effort to please, and in fear of being judged, the giver spends more money than he or she can afford
- The receiver is more focused on his or her own needs and wants than on the care the giver has taken.

The greatest gifts are not material gifts at all. They are expressed through the real time we choose to spend with one another, the genuine acknowledgment that we offer for things that are done for us, and our voiced recognition of the time, effort, and care involved in those loving gifts. There is a time-honored rhythm to gratitude. It is a three-step waltz of giving, receiving, and reciprocating.

QUIZ: HOW GRATEFUL IS YOUR ATTITUDE?

On a scale of 0 to 10, where are you on the Gr-Attitude scale? Try this quiz to get an overview of your approach to gratitude, and find out in which areas you could increase your gratitude or appreciation. Do it now and then again once you've worked through the activities. Has anything changed?

1. I look forward to each new day:

No					Sometimes					Yes
0	1	2	3	4	5	6	7	8	9	10

2. I try to look for the positive in every situation:

No					Sometimes					Yes
0	1	2	3	4	5	6	7	8	9	10

3. I prefer to think the best of people:

No					Sometimes					Yes
0	1	2	3	4	5	6	7	8	9	10

4. I find it easy to offer help to others:

No					Sometimes					Yes
0	1	2	3	4	5	6	7	8	9	10

5. I find it easy to accept help from others:

No					Sometimes					Yes
0	1	2	3	4	5	6	7	8	9	10

6. I would help a stranger who was in need:

No					Perhaps					Yes
0	1	2	3	4	5	6	7	8	9	10

7. I often actively feel grateful for my friends and/or my family:

No					Sometimes					Yes
0	1	2	3	4	5	6	7	8	9	10

8. There is so much in the world that is beautiful and to be thankful for:

No					Perhaps					Yes
0	1	2	3	4	5	6	7	8	9	10

9. I own everything I need to be happy:

No					Perhaps					Yes
0	1	2	3	4	5	6	7	8	9	10

10. Generally in life, I feel very contented:

No					Sometimes					Yes
0	1	2	3	4	5	6	7	8	9	10

Mostly 7–10 scores

Feeling thankful comes easily to you. Did you score 10/10 on many of these questions? Your levels of gratitude will shore up your life with resilience and perseverance and help you to feel happier every day.

Mostly 4–6 scores

Do you live life with a touch of cynicism? Do you prioritize work over spending time with your friends and family? It is possible that you are shutting out companionship and support that could enrich your life and make you happier.

Any 0–3 scores

Sometimes in life we become so overwhelmed with our troubles that we feel stuck and alone. If any of your scores are on the low side, please seek support from a friend or from a professional who could help you to shine a new light on your situation. There is much to feel grateful for in this evolving world of ours.

"DO NOT SPOIL WHAT YOU HAVE BY DESIRING WHAT YOU HAVE NOT; REMEMBER THAT WHAT YOU NOW HAVE WAS ONCE AMONG THE THINGS YOU ONLY HOPED FOR."

Epicurus (341–270 BCE)

WEEKLY ACTIVITIES

Discover gratitude week by week with a range of simple activities that you can easily incorporate into your everyday life. The note pages throughout can be used to record your thoughts and feelings at the end of each section, developing over time into your personal gratitude journal.

FIND THE GOOD THINGS IN YOUR LIFE

In week 1, you might be wondering, what is it you should feel thankful for? The easy answer is anything and everything—or anyone—that holds meaning for you and has an impact on your life, whether now or in the past.

You might feel thankful for something that you have experienced personally, or grateful for something that has happened to someone else. It could be something as simple as hearing a great new track on the radio or buying a new sweater, or as profound as being reunited with a friend, or hearing news of someone recovering from illness.

THIS WEEK...

Note down and reflect on some of the things you have to be thankful for:

People: your friends, family, neighbors, colleagues, kind strangers, teachers, past acquaintances, anyone who has inspired you. What kindnesses have you experienced recently? Whom are you grateful to have in your life? Who has offered you their trust or loyalty? Who has supported and helped you? Whom would you like to thank for past generosity or wisdom?

Places: home and what it means to you, vacation places that trigger wonderful memories, places of interest that inspire you, destinations that feed your imagination and dreams for the future.

Heritage: where you came from, your culture, traditions, and history.

Things: wonderful objects, clever design, amazing architecture: the joy of driving your car, enjoying a great movie or TV series, the comfort of your favorite chair after spending time away.

The natural world: the sky, sea, animals, birds, trees, plants, the weather, and landscape offer so much that inspires us and that we can be grateful for.

You: your uniqueness, your talents, foibles, friends, successes and failures, goals and achievements. When we live more consciously and more gratefully, we become more alive and alert to the potential of each moment.

WK 1
Dec 30 – Jan 5
2019   2020

REFLECT... ON THE GOOD THINGS
IN YOUR LIFE

LOOK FOR CONTRASTS

Gratitude flourishes in situations of contrast, perhaps because that is when we can see most clearly how fortunate we are. The beauty of a grateful attitude is that by focusing consciously on all we have to be grateful for, we create ever greater contrasts.

We begin to see that the world we have created could become even better, and so we seek ways to make that change happen.

- When it is dark, we appreciate the gift of light.
- When we are ill, we appreciate good health.
- When we are lonely, we appreciate our friends through their absence.
- When junk food is the only thing on the menu, we long for home cooking.
- When we are shocked by the horrors of war, we feel thankful for the safety of loved ones.
- When we see others struggle, we are more inclined to appreciate our own lives.
- When we are in despair, we move toward hope.

THIS WEEK...

Notice any situation this week that leads you to appreciate what you have in your life. Where possible, think about what you can do to improve a situation for someone else.

Week 2
Jan 6 - 12

REFLECT... ON ANY CONTRASTS
...D TO YOU FEELING GRATEFUL

8 -H
- 1500 Evarts NE

Article about
Homeless (Ness)
on DC streets
being evicted from
tent cities read
1.11.20   Claire
First childhood
memory
Passive but empt?
$ financial donations

PRACTICE THE POWER OF 3

There seems to be magic in the power of three. Three offers stability and balance: it is the base of the triangle, the third leg of the stool. Time is spoken about in divisions of three: past, present, and future. It is common to say that things happen in threes. Your day is made up of morning, afternoon, and evening. Spiritually, the number three has great significance.

Staying tuned in to the things that happen around you has great power and will increase in impact over time. You may find that your gratitude evolves a little like this:

1. One note of appreciation for a kindness.
2. One observation about the world around you.
3. One deeper thought.

A DAILY HABIT

The internationally renowned psychologist Professor Martin Seligman, director of the Penn Positive Psychology Center at Pennsylvania State University, recommends thinking of "three good things" about each day. He has proven that this simple action leads directly to an increase in well-being. Most of us can think of three things to be grateful for each day:

- How lucky that the sun shone all day today.
- The roses are looking fabulous and they smell astonishing.
- I am so glad I have finally arranged a date to meet my oldest friend.

As you develop the gratitude habit, you will discover that you go to greater depths with your thoughts. You may want to write more expressively about what the pathway to gratitude has shown you—and how it is transforming your thinking. See the examples on the opposite page.

Week 3

1. It was lovely of Jo to insist on picking me up when my car broke down earlier.

2. If I hadn't broken down I wouldn't have had the chance to spend so much time chatting with her and her daughter.

3. I am so relieved that the car broke down today and not on the way to work on Monday. It is interesting how often something good comes out of something annoying.

THIS WEEK...

Note down 3 things to be grateful for each day this week and then reflect and expand on them on the journal page overleaf.

Monday

_____

_____

_____

Tuesday

_____

_____

_____

Wednesday

_____

_____

_____

Thursday

_____

_____

_____

Friday

_____

_____

_____

Saturday

_____

_____

_____

Sunday

_____

_____

_____

REFLECT... ON YOUR POSITIVE FINDINGS
FOR EACH DAY

THERE'S A DONKEY IN HERE SOMEWHERE

The story goes that a mother once took her two sons to a psychiatrist. One boy was very pessimistic and the other very optimistic, and she wanted to understand why they were so different. The psychiatrist put the pessimistic boy in a room with some new toys, in the hope that they would make him feel happy. The optimistic boy, meanwhile, was put in a room filled with dung, to see whether that would curb his optimism. The psychiatrist then began to observe their reactions.

The boy with the new toys was not happy at all. Instead of welcoming the gifts, he feared that if he played with them he would break something and everything would be ruined. The psychiatrist then looked in on the boy with the pile of dung. He had found a shovel and was happily digging away with great energy. "What are you doing?" the psychiatrist asked.

"I am trying to find the donkey," answered the boy.

"What makes you think there is a donkey?" asked the psychiatrist.

"Well," said the boy, "with all this dung about, there must be one in here somewhere!"

The tale is, of course, apocryphal. It is very unlikely that any self-respecting doctor would put a child in a room with a pile of dung! However, the message is clear: optimism is good for us. It helps us to be grateful for what we have, and encourages us to see opportunities where a pessimist may see an obstacle.

Gratitude helps us to dig deep and find the positivity to overcome adversity in the most unlikely situations.

DISCOVER THE ABC OF OPTIMISM

Gratitude is a nourishing force that helps us to develop optimism and appreciation. The moment we say thank you or consciously show appreciation, negativity diminishes. However, it is hard to change our instinctive behavior after the event. If we want to alter the way we react to situations and become more grateful, we must consciously change the way we think before and during an event or occurrence.

Think about it as the **ABC** of optimism:

A is the trigger for the negative thoughts.

B is the behavior that has become an automatic response to that thought.

C is the consequence.

For example, each time your friend turns up late (**A**—the trigger) you start to feel resentment (**B**—the behavior). Rather than saying how you really feel, you say something sarcastic, which leads to an argument—which somehow turns out to be your fault (**C**—the consequence).

If, however, you know that her lateness will lead to you feeling resentful, you can be on the alert before **A** takes place, and prepare an alternative strategy. For example, you could say: "Shall we meet an hour later, as I know you find it hard to get here promptly from work?" Or, if you are feeling braver, "I need to let you know that when you turn up late I take it personally, and it feels as if you don't respect my feelings, which is why I get upset."

THIS WEEK...

Notice anything that triggers a negative thought and how it affects you. What can you do to break the cycle?

How did it make you feel afterward? Breaking the cycle will break the negativity, and feed an optimistic outlook instead.

REFLECT... ON BEING MORE OPTIMISTIC

OFFER THANKS THROUGH MEDITATION

In many spiritual practices prayer and meditation begin with the offering of thanks to the elders and ancestors whose lives and challenges have contributed to who we are today. In a whole-life meditation you might want to begin with the day you were born, and work through each year of your life to acknowledge important people and places, things that have happened, and those whom you appreciate.

The greatest value at first, however, is in focusing on the here and now. Take the time to focus, ideally in a place where you will not be disturbed. This might be at home, or in a park, or quietly on a train, while walking, or while traveling.

Allow your body to relax, from your toes to the top of your head. Pay special attention to letting go of the tension in different areas of your body, such as your feet, knees, shoulders, or jawline, by stretching, moving your body, or even yawning.

Be aware of whether you are starting from a mood of anger, frustration, or sadness—or whether you are already feeling positive and full of gratitude. Don't judge yourself for your feelings, or try to change them; just be aware of your state of mind.

Now breathe easily and naturally. Be patient with yourself, and begin to observe and recollect. Consider whom or what you are thankful for, and why. Depending on your state of mind, it may help to focus on a few details:

* The dawn chorus that I heard this morning.
* My warm gratitude toward the young boy who helped me yesterday.
* The bright yellow of the daffodils that are coming into flower.

Noticing and appreciating the positive elements of the world around you will have an uplifting effect. Starting off with small things leads quickly to thoughts of the big things:

* The love of my family.
* The kindness of my friends.
* The joy of watching my team score at the weekend.
* My relative health and the use of my body.
* The financial security that my job offers me.
* The memory of my mother's light and wisdom.

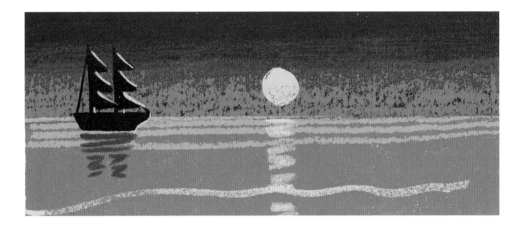

DEALING WITH DISTRACTIONS

If you become distracted, watch where your attention goes. Don't fight your thoughts, but see whether you can reframe them with gratitude. For example, if someone has been annoying you: "I am grateful for having X as my friend, even though he has been driving me insane! I know he has been going through a hard time. I will give him a call."

When I discussed this process with a friend of mine, she was confused about what or whom the gratitude was being directed at. She was wary of and uncomfortable with the uncertainty of abstract concepts such as thanking the universe. It really doesn't matter whom you thank, or how you do it. The person who will benefit most from your feelings of gratitude is you. However, when we value the wonder of the universe as a whole, it becomes much harder to feel upset about life's smaller irritations. From such a great height we can no longer see them, or feel them as acutely—and eventually they may even cease to matter.

THIS WEEK...

Many people find it difficult to find time to meditate. This week think about how you can fit meditation in your life. Maybe you could get up a little earlier (meditation really is a great start to the day!) or turn off the TV or your computer a little earlier each night and end the day with a relaxing meditation.

REFLECT... ON YOUR GRATITUDE MEDITATION

A FRANCISCAN BLESSING

(Thirteenth century)

May you be blessed with discomfort at easy answers, half-truths,
and superficial relationships—so that you may live deep
within your heart.

May you be blessed with anger at injustice, oppression, and exploitation of people—
so that you may work for justice, freedom, and peace.

May you be blessed with tears shed for those who suffer pain, rejection, hunger,
and war—so that you may reach out your hand to comfort them and turn
their pain to joy.

May you be blessed with enough foolishness to believe that you can make a difference
to the world—so that you can do what others claim cannot be done, to bring
justice and kindness to our children and to the poor.

BE GRATEFUL FOR HEALTHY FOOD

Nourishing your body in a healthy and thankful way begins with the shopping list, carries on with your chosen route around the store (we all know which aisles we should feel less grateful for!), and ends up at the checkout.

As anyone who has ever consciously changed their eating habits will know, the key to eating healthily is forward planning. Some people find that focusing anew on the beauty and color of fresh vegetables and thinking consciously about the goodness and nutrients can help them to drop the chocolate and swap saturated fats for healthy options. The majority of us, however, often struggle with following the healthy path, especially when under pressure.

- Feel grateful for the foods you enjoy that are healthy, and eat more of them. For example, if you enjoy the sweetness of fruit, it can be helpful to have some on standby to distract your taste buds before you head off to the store.
- Feel thankful that sometimes, when we think we are hungry, we are simply bored, anxious, or thirsty. Try having a savory or hot drink, or doing something that is active and different for a few minutes, and wait for the craving to pass.
- Feel delighted that our bodies prefer to heal and get well if they can. If you focus on swapping unhealthy patterns for healthy ones, it will get easier to maintain your new lifestyle.
- Finally, "think gratitude" for your new plan of action as you enter each store. That way, you will be less likely to overspend or to buy food that is less nourishing and that you will feel less grateful for later.

THIS WEEK...

Be mindful of the food you prepare and eat. Take time to appreciate how it smells and tastes. Chew slowly and eat away from any distractions such as the TV or your phone. Focus on how healthy foods are nourishing your body and be thankful.

Week 6

REFLECT... ON EATING A HEALTHY DIET

February
8—14

_____

_____

_____

_____

_____

_____

_____

_____

_____

_____

_____

_____

_____

_____

_____

_____

_____

_____

_____

_____

_____

TUNE IN TO YOUR WORDS

The enemies of gratitude are negative thoughts, which influence our choice of words and then our actions. Pay attention to how you react and the words you use when faced with disappointment, or when things don't quite go to plan.

Our use of language tells us a great deal about our state of mind: "I wish," "I regret," "If only," "I should have," "I wanted to," "I am fed up," "Why should I," "I can't ..." Oh, the joy of "shouldawouldacoulda." All these phrases are energy depleters that take away our personal power and deplete our positivity. Over time, as we blame other people or bad luck for our circumstances, we begin to feel powerless. It may become harder to feel joy or to act spontaneously, and difficult to forgive those around us for being less than perfect, or the world for not living up to our expectations. The natural power of gratitude, however, is such that it is also quite easy to adjust our responses and reframe our experience in a more positive light, if we choose to do so.

THE LANGUAGE OF GRATITUDE

By contrast with complaints and regrets, the language of gratitude has a feel-good factor that tends to be infectious and lifts others, too. Giving positive voice to your feelings gives them additional power, although it can be challenging and emotional on occasion. Make it a habit to say "thank you" for the simple things as well as the big things in life. Gratitude is a gift that reciprocates in goodwill. You will always get back as much as or more than you give—and your positivity and appreciative attitude will subtly influence others to become more positive, without anyone realizing it.

THIS WEEK...

Try thinking to yourself, or writing down, or saying out loud in a private moment each day:

- I am thankful for...
- I am glad that...
- I appreciate...
- How kind that...

REFLECT... ON YOUR CHOICE OF WORDS

REMEMBER
POSITIVE WORDS
=
POSITIVE
ATTITUDE

FIND YOUR POLLYANNA

The original gratitude guru must be Pollyanna, a fictional character in the American classic children's story of the same name by Eleanor H. Porter. Unfailingly (and, some would say, unrelentingly) positive and cheery, Pollyanna is taught by her father to look for the good in everything and to be "glad" for every obstacle she faces in life, because something positive will be revealed in every situation.

When Pollyanna is sent to live with her strict and emotionally absent Aunt Polly after her father dies, she focuses on playing "the glad game" in the face of many trials and tribulations. In classic Hollywood style, her positive outlook eventually melts every heart. The Pollyanna stories became known as "The Glad Books," and the name Pollyanna is now synonymous with an extreme kind of naïve and boundless positivity.

The first Pollyanna story is unsettling by modern standards, even if the eventual outcome is positive. Pollyanna's cloak of gratitude protects her from the awareness that she is being deliberately and cruelly starved of care and affection by her aunt. However, the moral of the tale is very clear: even in adversity, when we have lost everything, living life with a glad heart and gratitude can help us to retain a sense of self-determination and optimism about the future. Eleanor Porter would have a lot in common with the positive psychology movement if she were alive today.

"THERE IS SOMETHING ABOUT EVERYTHING
THAT YOU CAN BE GLAD ABOUT, IF YOU KEEP
HUNTING LONG ENOUGH TO FIND IT."

Eleanor H. Porter (1868–1920)

THIS WEEK...

On a scale of 1 to 10, what do you think is your Pollyanna-style "Gladness" score?

1 2 3 4 5 6 7 8 9 10
Grumbling Aunt Polly   Gladly Pollyanna

Are you somewhere between 5 and 10? Are you Pollyanna—a fully paid-up optimist, glad to be alive and grateful for everything that happens to you? Do you more often find yourself at the lower end of the scale—more Aunt Polly than Pollyanna?

Most of us are in the middle, around 5 or 6: full of enthusiasm one minute and easily let down the next; programmed to believe that everything will get better, but not beyond moaning a great deal when things don't work out as planned.

REFLECT... ON YOUR POLLYANNA SCORE

GRATITUDE IN PRACTICE

Maria was in her forties when, through a series of unexpected circumstances, she took in a homeless young woman, who was pregnant. Maria had very little in the way of financial resources, but she hadn't stopped to think twice about offering the young woman a home.

After taking advice she was told that some financial support was likely to be available. The advice turned out to be misguided, however, and no external funds were available. Determined to act with love and compassion, Maria decided to look her lack of funds in the face and turn it into a gift. Each week she handed the young woman an allowance and told her that it was her contribution to their mutual household budget. She was to choose for herself the food she would like to eat, and prepare several meals for them both each week. The transformation was remarkable. The young woman not only treated the allowance with respect and bought food carefully, but also discovered a talent for creative cooking that she didn't know she had. When the baby arrived she had the confidence to know that she could prepare meals and manage a budget. Maria's loving kindness was met with the kind of gratitude that makes a friend for life.

"YOUR DIFFICULTIES DO NOT COME TO
DESTROY YOU, BUT TO HELP YOU DISCOVER
YOUR HIDDEN POTENTIAL."

Adapted from a quote by
A.P.J. Abdul Kalam (1931–2015), 11th President of India

TURN A NEGATIVE INTO A POSITIVE

Turning bad into good is not always easy or possible—especially in the short term—
but it can definitely help to look consciously at the brighter side of a situation.

If you've had one of those days, and everything seems to have gone wrong, it can be
hard to know how to show gratitude. Instead of focusing on the bad things, spend time
thinking about what else happened to you. You might be surprised!

Gratitude has the capacity to improve our sense of well-being and optimism, which
can gradually help us to let go of or make sense of negative feelings or memories.

Looking on the bright side: "Although I am terrified by the idea of the medical
treatment, I am hugely relieved that I now know what is wrong with me. I am starting
to allow myself to hope that I can get through this."

Being completely honest with yourself: "Although I am devastated that I have been
made redundant, I must admit that I had been thinking of leaving that job for a while,
and perhaps this period may give me time to retrain."

Acknowledging the dark side: "I feel grateful for the memory of the arguments we had
because it helps me to know in my heart that it is better that we have parted."

Be aware that gratitude does not thrive in a situation of servitude or beholdenness.
There are some circumstances where the right thing to do is not to accept or feel
grateful for your situation—and instead to feel thankful that you have free will to bring
about change, with the help of others, too, as necessary.

THIS WEEK...

Write about a negative situation you have been struggling with and then find a positive from it. You may find it helps to talk it through with someone close to you—other people can sometimes view things more objectively and throw a positive light on things.

REFLECT... ON FINDING THE POSITIVE

BE THANKFUL FOR HOME COMFORTS

Many of us get caught up in feelings of dissatisfaction with our homes and have a long list of what we'd like to change. Here's how to love where we live.

It's easy to take our home environment for granted and focus on what we don't like about it rather than what we do. Most of us want more – a bigger garden, more light, updated furniture. A browse though an Instagram feed packed with lust-worthy, immaculate houses can leave yours feeling somewhat lacking. A recent survey of Londoners found that 50 percent felt unhappy with their homes after scrolling through social media. Remember that what you see online is rarely the whole picture—there is likely to be a bundle of laundry just out of shot of any pristine scene!

Adjust your focus from craving change and home improvements to striving to find contentedness with what you have—take a moment to admire a favorite bowl or mug, or when loading the washing machine, pause and reflect on the fact that we live in a time of modern conveniences where these things are at our fingertips.

"Gratitude can turn a meal into a feast, a house into a home,'" says author Melody Beattie. Appreciate what turns your house into a home—is it a comfy armchair, a view of a tree-lined street outside, or the kitchen that forms the center of your family's lives?

A glance around the streets will act as a reminder, too, that there are plenty out there less fortunate. Remind yourself of your good fortune.

THIS WEEK...

Hygge is a Danish concept, and roughly translates as creating coziness, warmth, and happiness though embracing simple pleasures. Here are three ways to boost your well-being and take pleasure in your home:

- Light candles and find comfort and relaxation in their flickering dance.
- Invite friends round and appreciate your connection and togetherness.
- Dig out a soft blanket, snuggly socks, and make your favorite hot drink.

REFLECT... ON YOUR HOME COMFORTS

BE THANKFUL FOR YOUR BODY

There are many ways that you can show appreciation for the gift of your health and your body. It may sound obvious, but the key to success is to do things that you are drawn toward and that you enjoy. Here are a few ideas.

How many hours, days, or weeks have we all spent regretting that our bodies have some perceived flaw? The physical frame that you call a body carries you, enables you to breathe, and keeps your heart beating, even—within limits—when it is mistreated with the wrong kind of food, unhealthy behavior, or negative thoughts.

It may be time to show gratitude for your physical self by giving your body more of what it really needs to flourish and maintain good health. Take the pledge to give thanks for your body every day.

GIVE BACK TO YOUR BODY

If you have been neglecting exercise and need to get started again, you may like to consider one or more of the following to begin with:

- Go for a meaningful walk each day—around the block, to a nearby park, or to somewhere new. (Borrow a friend's dog if that will help to motivate you!) Notice how your body feels as you breathe in the air and feel the wind on your skin. Realize that you really are miraculous—and that is worth being grateful for.

- Music is one of the most incredible gifts of all. Our bodies are designed for movement, so who can resist getting up to dance when the sound matches our mood? Dancing is exercise and pure enjoyment rolled into one. Whether dancing in the kitchen to the radio, or letting go in full party mode, dancing "gives back" to your body while music feeds your soul—the perfect way to feel thankful for being alive.

Week 11

- Treat yourself to an occasional massage or reflexology session. In the right hands a treatment will help to balance your body and get rid of tension, so that your blood flows more readily, your gut works more healthily, and you feel revitalized. Feel gratitude for the expertise of the professional who gives you your treatment, and appreciate consciously how much better you are afterward.

- If you have access to a garden, spending 20 minutes or so a day weeding, planting, and nurturing will reap great rewards—for you as well as the plants. Take time to see what is growing, how things have changed since yesterday, the shapes, colors, scents, and behavior of every small thing, from an opening flower to the buzzing circuit of a bee.

- If you feel more adventurous, offering gratitude to others by taking part in a sponsored walk, half-marathon, or other challenge for a greater cause can help to get you focused, motivated, and fit at the same time.

THIS WEEK...

List three things that you like about your body and would like to give thanks for. Aim for:

1. One note of appreciation

_____

_____

_____

_____

2. One observation

_____

_____

_____

3. One deeper thought

_____

_____

_____

REFLECT... ON APPRECIATING YOUR BODY

_____

_____

_____

_____

_____

_____

_____

_____

_____

_____

_____

_____

_____

_____

_____

_____

_____

_____

_____

_____

GRATITUDE BLESSING

This blessing has been inspired by Jack Kornfield, a Buddhist practitioner and teacher. His work consistently explains the rich value that such practice offers us in developing a more open-hearted, joyful, and grateful approach to life.

Let yourself sit quietly and in a relaxed fashion. Take a deep breath and then let go. Let your heart feel easy. Listen to your breath as you breathe in and out quietly and naturally. Allow your body to let go of all tension and become ready to receive this blessing:

I offer my gratitude to the universe and all that is in it, for
the friends I have been given;
the family I have been given;
the joy of life that I have been given;
the state of health and well-being that I have been given;
the neighbors that I have been given;
the teachers that I have been given;
the wisdom that I have been given;
the beauty of this earth, and the animals and birds that we have
all been given;
my life and all that I have been given.

Now continue to breathe in and out gently. Picture someone you care about, and think about them as they go about their daily life—and about the happiness and success you wish for them. With each breath, offer them your thanks from the bottom of your heart:

May you always have joy in your heart.
May you always enjoy good fortune.
May your happiness continue to increase.
May you always have peace and well-being on this earth.

BE MORE EXPRESSIVE

Many people find it difficult to express their emotions, but it seems that the level to which we share our gratitude can have a positive impact on our well-being.

In a research project a group of volunteers were asked to complete a happiness questionnaire. They were then asked to identify someone who had made an important impact on their lives, and to whom they had reason to feel very grateful. Each person was then asked to write an expression of thanks to that individual, in the form of a letter. It was an intense exercise for all involved, and everyone assumed that once they had completed the assignment, that would be the end of the session. Far from it, however. Each participant was asked to telephone the person they wished to thank, there and then—and to read out to them the letter they had written.

The effect was extraordinary. Quite apart from the emotional impact on the person who received the unexpected expression of heartfelt gratitude at the other end of the phone line, there was a measurable and positive outcome for the person who was offering their thanks, too. When the volunteers retook the questionnaire, their scores increased by an average of 90 percent! (In contrast, those who had written letters but had not phoned scored an increase of 20 percent. Still extremely positive—but not as remarkable.) It seems that gratitude is a very fast-acting emotion, and one that has an immediate impact on our well-being.

THIS WEEK...

Consider who you'll go the extra mile to thank this week. If you can, try doing what the people in the research study (see above) did. Write the letter and then call the person and read it out to them. Reflect on how doing this made you feel.

REFLECT... ON WAYS OF EXPRESSING YOUR GRATITUDE

BE THANKFUL FOR MUSIC

Music can be a powerful tool to boost well-being, if we take the time
to celebrate and appreciate it.

Music has the power to alter our emotional state, whether it's a song that immediately
uplifts us and provides a burst of energy, or a tune that triggers a poignant memory
from the past. Experts believe that if we actively engage with music, it can provide even
more of a boost to well-being. Studies show that music can actually release a feel-good
chemical in our brains—researchers at McGill University in Canada found that
dopamine was produced at moments of peak enjoyment.

Be mindful of how particular types of music impact your mood and use that to
your advantage. Play a song that lifts your spirits when you're feeling flat, or one that
calms you when life is fraught.

Take the time to properly listen to and enjoy the music you love as opposed to
simply having it as background noise. Be glad, too, of the variety of music out there
and explore different genres—ask friends what they like, actively seek out new
material, and expand your horizons.

If you find you enjoy singing, you may want to consider signing up to a choir
as a way to appreciate music? A communal singalong can be the ultimate feel-
good pastime and you don't need to have the best voice in the world to join in.

THIS WEEK...

Make a point of singing out loud this week—
perhaps in the shower or as you're driving
along. Turn off the TV and sing along to your
favorite tunes. If you have children, join in
with them for a sing-song. Take a moment
to appreciate the positive effect that singing
and music have on your well-being.

REFLECT... ON WHAT MUSIC BRINGS TO YOUR LIFE

BE THANKFUL FOR BOOKS

Take a moment to be glad of curling up with a good book, one that can transport you to a different place and lower stress levels.

Getting lost in a novel can be a great joy and is one that is worthy of pausing to appreciate. Experts believe that reading can have a positive impact on well-being. "One sheds one's sickness in books," D.H. Lawrence once wrote, and research shows that just six minutes of reading can reduce stress levels by two-thirds. Psychologists believe this is because the mind has to fully focus on reading and the distraction of being transported to a literary world eases tensions.

So next time you have 10 minutes to spare, rather than reaching for your phone, grab a book instead and be glad of the escapism from everyday stresses and notice if you feel your heart rate slow. We take it for granted, but even just the ability to read can be a source of gratitude, given that 775 million people in the world are illiterate.

Bookshops can be a wonderful way to appreciate books and browse, if you have time to spare. But you don't need to spend a fortune on new books—be thankful for libraries, where you can read novels and try out new authors for free.

If a book has helped you to de-stress, to expand yourself, or has simply been a riveting read, show your gratitude by passing it on to a friend or colleague or give it to charity. Taking the time to pass it on will help cement the feeling of appreciation.

THIS WEEK...

Pass on the gift of literature by offering to read aloud to someone—maybe an older relative or neighbor—who may find it difficult to read themselves. Sharing a story, poem, or even magazine feature may increase your own appreciation and the act of kindness is likely to bring the recipient comfort and joy, too.

REFLECT... ON WHAT BOOKS BRING TO YOUR LIFE

PRACTICE PATIENCE

Many people feel they are living life in the fast lane, with insufficient time to "stop and stare." When we rush, we prevent ourselves from having the time to fully appreciate all that we are experiencing. There is a danger that we can become victims of circumstance rather than living consciously.

Sometimes we need time to understand the gift we have been given or to grasp the true impact of what is happening in life. Developing patience can allow time to refocus, or to see that there is benefit even in adverse experiences. Living life more slowly and taking time to notice how we are feeling increases our sense of awareness in the broadest sense. We start to pay greater attention and can choose to develop a sense of gratitude for other people and for our world.

DELAYED GRATIFICATION

The ability to delay gratification in childhood has long been associated with a greater capacity for material success in later life. However, factors that are allied with this are patience and gratitude. In a study in the United States, participants were given the choice between receiving an immediate cash reward or waiting up to 12 months for a larger windfall of as much as $100. It turned out that those who showed the least patience and gratitude tended to claim payment at the $18 mark. The more grateful people held out, on average, until the amount reached $30.

    The conclusion was that when we feel thankful for what we already have, we are less likely to give in to the impulse for immediate gratification.

THIS WEEK...

Notice when you are rushing through your day and take a moment to slow down or even stop.

Reflect on how this more patient approach to life helps you to appreciate and live in the moment more.

REFLECT... ON BEING MORE PATIENT

_____
_____
_____
_____
_____
_____
_____
_____
_____
_____
_____
_____
_____
_____
_____
_____
_____

BEING THANKFUL FOR YOUR PARTNER

Professor Sara Algoe has spent many years researching the role of gratitude in relationships. In a study of 47 couples between the ages of 24 and 40 (who had been together for an average of five years), she found a connection between being actively grateful and feeling more positive about each other. During the study, over the course of 30 consecutive days, some of the couples were asked to spend time together each day chatting about everyday things, while other couples were asked to spend time each day expressing gratitude to each other for the little things that had happened. The couples were also asked to complete a daily questionnaire, to find out how they were feeling about their relationship on a scale from 1 to 9. For example, in answer to the question "Today our relationship was …," the couples had to answer from 1 ("terrible") to 9 ("terrific").

Rather wonderfully, Professor Algoe discovered that in contrast to the couples who were just passing the time of day, the couples who were giving each other positive messages of gratitude found that their relationships had strengthened as a result. Receiving gratitude had made each person more likely to feel appreciated and therefore more motivated to express gratitude to the other person, too.

All too often in a long-term relationship, there is a gradual increase in finding fault and noticing what is lacking, rather than looking actively for what is good about each other.

When we *find* reasons to be grateful and feel positive about each other, and also remind each other that we appreciate each other, we start to appreciate ourselves more, too. Over time, this kind of positivity makes the individuals in a couple feel more confident about being "good at" relationships, and reinforces their feelings for each other. Although the research is not definitive, the results seem to show that a daily dose of appreciation and positivity *binds* us together more happily.

Of course, both people must be equally committed to expressing gratitude, and it also depends on how we express appreciation. Our tone of voice and the level of sincerity are all important. The memory expert Tony Buzan often remarks that we remember beginnings, endings, and points of difference more clearly than any other element within a conversation. So, no matter what you have discussed with your partner, if you start and end by expressing appreciation and gratitude, that is what he or she is most likely to remember.

"FIND. REMIND. BIND."

Professor Sara Algoe PhD, University of North Carolina

BE THANKFUL FOR TECHNOLOGY

The digital world can be a place of connectedness, communication, and entertainment, if entered into wisely. Technology has its down side, but it's important to recognize and be thankful for what it brings to our lives.

It's undeniable that being tied to our digital devices 24/7 is not usually a path to happiness and fulfilment, but technology is here to stay and, used wisely and mindfully, has a multitude of benefits that we can be thankful for. Used without consideration it may encourage social isolation, but it can also enrich our lives by bringing us together and helping us communicate with loved ones.

And while playing computer games late into the night may negatively impact your health, appreciate that there are ways that your health can be boosted through technology, too—for example, there are apps that help you monitor your heart rate and blood pressure, others that count your steps and encourage activity, and those that guide you through a relaxing meditation.

The online world can boost our brain power. We have access to a wealth of information at our fingertips, more than ever before.

Be grateful, too, for the choice of entertainment available to us—we can choose TV programs on demand, or find exactly what we're craving at the touch of a button.

THIS WEEK...

To get the most from technology and appreciate it, try opting out sometimes, too. Here are some simple, achievable ways to reduce your tech time:

- Have regular tech breaks and tune in to what's going on around you.
- Do something active in the fresh air such as a walk in the park or arrange to meet a friend for a coffee so you interact with people.
- Set yourself a maximum daily screen time, such as an hour in the evening to check social media, to avoid mindlessly dipping in and out of it all day.

REFLECT... ON HOW YOU BENEFIT FROM TECHNOLOGY

MAKING TIME FOR GRATITUDE

We all lead busy lives, so "making time" for additional activities is not always an option. The beauty of living life more thankfully is that small changes in everyday thoughts and outlook can reap big rewards—with no need to find "extra" time in your daily routine.

THE POWER OF THANK YOU

It is all too easy to take those whom we love and who care for us for granted. Saying "thank you" regularly to members of your family for everyday things has been shown to strengthen bonds and help to increase the sense of connection and togetherness.

GETTING FROM A TO B

Daily commuters are masters at "going inward" to create some mental space between themselves and their fellow travelers. Many wear headphones or focus on their cell phones or tablets. The journey to work is a natural time to start to "think more thankfully." Stuck in traffic? Squashed on the subway? Missed the bus? Late for work? Once you have accepted that you can do nothing about the situation, there is scope to divert your attention away from feeling irritated or anxious and toward the more helpful feeling of conscious gratitude.

IN THE TUB OR SHOWER

Whether you are in and out of the shower in five minutes or enjoy luxuriating for longer, clearing your mind while you clean your body is a great combination. Many people find they have their most creative thoughts while relaxing in the tub, so it is a valuable time for contemplating gratitude, too.

WHEN WAKING UP OR BEFORE YOU GO TO SLEEP

There is a lot to be said for keeping a notebook by your bed. Many of us have our clearest or most creative thoughts just before we go to sleep or in half-slumber before waking. Gratitude for past kindnesses, memories of loving support, or thoughts of a gesture we could make to someone who is in need or has been generous: these things may come to mind more readily when we are not focusing on them directly. Make a note before the thoughts slip away.

"A GRATEFUL HEART IS A MAGNET
FOR MIRACLES."

Anonymous

PLAN SOME GIFT-GIVING

Personal gifts have come to symbolize feelings, so a very basic item can become imbued with meaning if it has been chosen with love and care. A rock collected on a clifftop walk may summon up memories of a special day; a single rose may be given in full awareness of all that it symbolizes; and a graduation gift may increase in emotional value as the years go by, as it represents a rite of passage and the love and respect of others.

PAYING ATTENTION—THE DILEMMA OF CHOOSING A GIFT

A beautiful parcel can be a joy to behold and the unwrapping a moment to be treasured. When choosing a gift, the more important the person is to you, the greater your wish will be to come up with something ideal, meaningful, memorable, and possibly original, too. So deciding to give someone a gift is about much more than choosing a present. When we put time aside to focus on someone who holds meaning for us, we begin to reflect on ourselves, too:

- Would she like this?
- Does he have one?
- If I get it wrong, will he think I don't care?
- Will he want one?
- Why don't I know more about her taste?
- Will it suit her?

As adults, we find it easier to give than to receive, so it is important to respect one another's needs, and to consider our wish to give from the receiver's perspective as well as our own. Good intentions swiftly turn to panic when too much is riding on getting it "right." Each time we doubt ourselves, we are really asking: Why haven't I paid greater attention?

Whatever the style of giving and whatever the occasion, it will always be the "right" gift when we give with good heart and have devoted some thought to our decision. If in doubt, ask! Not every gift has to be a surprise.

WHAT KIND OF GIFT-GIVER ARE YOU?

- Do you spend hours choosing the "right" gift for every person and occasion?
- Do you spend time wrapping the gift beautifully, especially when you feel the contents are modest?
- Do you give money instead of a gift for fear of "getting it wrong?"

You may decide that giving a gift serves no purpose, and that a kindly written card or a meaningful call has more value.

It sometimes feels as if there are a lot of rules and rituals surrounding the act of giving. Some are fun, and become part of an occasion, but others may be embedded in a bygone time that has very little relevance today. More often than not, the gift of celebration is a gift in itself—it is the presence of friends and loved ones rather than presents that most of us prefer.

THIS WEEK...

Think about upcoming birthdays or Christmas and plan how you might change your gift-giving habits. Reflect on the people you are giving to, thinking about what they bring to your life and how you can show appreciation with a gift.

REFLECT... ON HOW YOU GIVE GIFTS

_____

_____

_____

_____

_____

_____

_____

_____

_____

_____

_____

_____

_____

_____

_____

_____

_____

_____

_____

_____

_____

_____

GIVING AWAY THE PAST

"I love my books and had built up a substantial collection—many from college and school days," says Tammy. "The idea of giving any of them away was anathema to me. They were part of who I am—or so I thought.

When I came to move home in my fifties, I started to browse through some of the books as I packed them. I realized that not only was the typeface far too small for my aging eyes, it was also the first time I had leafed through the pages in 30 years! I decided to take radical action before I had a chance to change my mind. I photographed the books' spines so I could re-order favorite titles online, and took several boxes of books to goodwill stores. The charity volunteers were grateful to have such a useful windfall, my husband was grateful that our removal storage charges would not be quite as high, and as an added bonus our grandchildren were very proud that I had finally discovered the joy of reading books online and had made it into the twenty-first century. A positive result all round."

"YOU HAVE NOT LIVED TODAY UNTIL YOU HAVE
DONE SOMETHING FOR SOMEONE WHO CAN
NEVER REPAY YOU."

John Bunyan (1628–1688)

MAKE A PERSONAL GIFT

Giving a gift is a special way to show gratitude, and need not be expensive. Choosing something with wit, care, originality, or attention to detail has far more value than a luxury label.

Call on the skills you have or learn some new skills to create something special.

- Take a special photograph, and get family, friends, or colleagues to sign the mount. It will immediately become precious, even before you put it in a frame.

- Buy real ribbon made of natural fiber to tie up your parcels. It often costs no more than synthetic ribbon, and it makes your gift look extra-special. If possible, deliver the packages in person.

- Pass on a favorite book, DVD, or CD. It will mean even more to the recipient to know that it was yours and that you loved it. To make the gift extra-special, include some treats that your friend or relative can enjoy while watching or listening (a pair of snuggle socks or a big candy bar, perhaps).

- Create a simple posy of handpicked flowers, grasses, or leaves, containing an odd number of each element, such as three or five.

- Give something away. Most of us own far more than we need. As adults we may be hanging on to items that were precious to us in younger years—clothes or toys or paraphernalia from long-lost hobbies—but that someone else could be gaining pleasure from now. Giving things away is enormously liberating, especially when you know that objects from your past are adding joy to someone's present.

THIS WEEK...

Try baking a cake. This is a simple way to show love to someone and once they know it's made with love it won't really matter what it looks (or tastes!) like. If you're not up to making a cake, try homemade cookies instead. If you're already a confident baker, set yourself a new baking challenge.

REFLECT... ON HOW IT FELT TO GIVE A PERSONAL GIFT

_____
_____
_____
_____
_____
_____
_____
_____
_____
_____
_____
_____
_____
_____
_____
_____
_____
_____

GIVE SOMETHING AWAY

When we give to others, we feel better about ourselves, and when we reciprocate the giving makes us feel emotionally in balance. There is giving and there is receiving, but it is in reciprocation that the magic happens. That is where human connection lies, and where there is equality in all things.

Imagine that you are on your way to buy groceries. A middle-aged man is near the entrance of the store, playing a few notes—badly—on a penny whistle, his cap on the ground to invite donations. He is dressed scruffily and appears not to have bathed in a while. Some people do not notice; some do not wish to see. Others see but are filled with fear and so do not approach him, although he is not dangerous. Occasionally someone pauses to offer him a few coins for his cap.

Each time someone speaks to him or gives him something, the man thanks them, sincerely and profusely—which means they walk away feeling good about themselves, even though he still does not have anywhere near enough money for an evening meal or a bed for the night, or even a drink, if that is his choice. When you watch more closely you notice that it is not the people with shopping carts piled high with purchases who are giving to the man, it is those who are moved by compassion and appear not to have much themselves, or an older person who seems alone, or a young person who has not yet learned to judge someone for their weaknesses.

THIS WEEK...

Tune into your generosity and think about what you could give away: perhaps a possession that you were thinking of putting on eBay to raise a small amount of income?

Or you could simply make a donation or give of your time. How did giving something away make you feel?

REFLECT... ON GIVING SOMETHING AWAY

RECEIVING AND RECIPROCATING

When someone gives a gift or gives of themselves, someone else receives and accepts what that person wished to share. Giving and receiving are the yin and yang of the exchange. Neither can exist without the other. It is a balanced ritual that extends back beyond the dawn of the world's religions.

There are few things in life that can lift our spirits more than hearing from someone we care about. Receiving letters, telephone calls, gifts, kind words, or symbols of love and recognition help to cement our feeling of belonging and being cared for. Receiving is also about gaining wisdom; about tuning in to the world around us and its impact on our senses; about noticing beauty in all its forms; and about appreciating the existence of other creatures who share this planet. Occasionally it involves feeling emotionally vulnerable. Receiving is not always straightforward.

Most of all, receiving is about acceptance. When someone offers you a present, they are truly offering you their presence, too. The gift becomes a symbol of your friendship, acquaintance, or other relationship. They have given you not only a gift, but also their time, attention, and care. Take time to savor it. Adjust your human antennae for a moment and tune in to the person who is paying you this compliment. What does their gesture tell you about them? How does their kindness reflect on you? Have you the generosity of spirit to let someone truly enjoy the moment of giving?

Reciprocation is all about maintaining a balance. If we receive without giving, we may feel lesser versions of ourselves; if our generosity is refused, we may feel rejected. For the dance to work in harmony we must be willing to receive as well as to give, to accept thanks as well as offer praise, and to be ready to offer our support to those who need help, simply because we are in a position where we can.

There is also the tricky area of feeling beholden, or the feelings of anger or resentment that may arise when receiving a gift or generous gesture suggests that the gift is being given for a less than straightforward reason, and that therefore something about the exchange is out of balance.

Thankfulness is not always an easy or a natural emotion. It can be difficult to feel grateful when facing intense hardship. Sometimes previous experiences trigger emotions that block the capacity for giving or receiving, and there seems to be little reason to feel appreciation. Reciprocation is not always direct. A kindness given to one person may be "passed on" via a kind act to another instead.

"WE CANNOT HOLD A TORCH TO LIGHT ANOTHER PERSON'S PATH WITHOUT SHINING LIGHT TO GUIDE OUR OWN WAY TOO."

Anonymous

CREATE MEMENTOES OF GRATITUDE

In years gone by, people made memory quilts—they sewed and embroidered their family stories into the fabric of the quilt. While you may not have the time or the skills to do this, there are other ways you can make meaningful mementoes.

VISUAL REMINDERS

Keeping photographs, cards, and postcards on a pinboard or on your fridge will remind you of the key people in your life, for whom you have heartfelt appreciation. Most people build these up over time, but in our increasingly digital world, printed reminders are fewer and farther between. Nowadays people are more like to make a digital photo album or Facebook page. Creating a place where everyone in the family can post their memories and share their stories can be a tremendous source of enjoyment that is appreciated by everyone and has the potential to be kept and shared forever. Memory books and photo collages are a wonderful way to capture history in the making.

SHARING STORIES

Getting together to share memories and stories, rather like creating a quilt, can keep memories alive and bring about a new sense of gratitude and connectedness. Everyone will have their own memory of growing up within your family. It can be fun to ask everyone to contribute their thoughts—and to write down a favorite story, a reason for gratitude, or what they like best about being in your family.

THIS WEEK...

Find the time to go through your recent photos and create something with them. If you can do this with other family members, it might make it even more rewarding and enjoyable. Share your creation with those people you are thankful for.

REFLECT... ON SPECIAL MEMORIES

_____

_____

_____

_____

_____

_____

_____

_____

_____

_____

_____

_____

_____

_____

_____

_____

_____

_____

_____

_____

_____

MAKE A GRATITUDE JAR

Create a personal pot of gratitude with ideas of ways to say thank you. This can be a real jar or a metaphorical jar, depending on whether you want a physical reminder or whether the act of contemplating the jar is enough to focus your thoughts.

The gratitude jar is a place where you can keep the names of the people you feel grateful toward and want to spend time with or write to or thank, as well as ideas and suggestions for expressions of thankfulness.

RANDOM GRATITUDE METHOD

Add the names of those you wish to thank on pieces of paper of one color, and ways to say thank you on pieces of paper of another color. Choose two pieces of paper, one of each color, to marry up ideas for giving. Be aware that choosing "Great Aunt Millie" and "Sky-dive treat" may not be the ideal combination!

FOCUSED GRATITUDE METHOD

The pot is the ideal place to turn all your guilty "shoulds" into positive action—write down specific ideas and choose one at random every so often. For example:

- Take Lily to the mall this weekend.
- Bake Tom a birthday cake this year.
- Phone Maud to find out about her health.

THIS WEEK...

Start as you mean to go on. Create your jar and aim to complete at least one of the actions.

Set yourself a goal of when you will select your next action from the gratitude jar.

REFLECT... ON HOW IT FELT TO MAKE YOUR GRATITUDE JAR

PERFECT YOUR THANK-YOU LETTERS

Why are thank-you letters so difficult to write? After a great day out, or the first time you use a wonderful gift, your letter should write itself, but the best of us can struggle to find the right words.

A tradition for centuries, the thank-you letter gives joy to the recipient as barely any other communication does. Sadly, it is a common misconception that thank-you letters are the preserve of the older generation and we now live in a world without letters, where texting and emailing have taken over our lives. According to research, a third of people aged under 35 have never written a letter or card to a loved one. In this digital age, it is perhaps more important than ever that we pass on to our children the art of writing a thank-you letter. By doing so we teach them a key life skill—that taking the time and effort to properly say thank you is a way of valuing others.

REWARDS

As well as the joy it brings to the person receiving the letter, writing a thank-you card or letter can be immensely pleasurable. Deciding on the words focuses your thoughts and strengthens your happy memories of the event or appreciation of a gift; and the finished piece is a small gesture of thanks in return for the joy you have been given.

THIS WEEK...

Instead of dropping a friend or family member a text or email this week to say thanks, make or choose a card and pop it in the post. It takes more effort but you will enjoy the reward of doing it.

REFLECT... ON WAYS YOU CAN PROPERLY SHOW YOUR THANKS TO OTHERS

_____

_____

_____

_____

_____

_____

_____

_____

_____

_____

_____

_____

_____

_____

_____

_____

_____

_____

GIVE THANKS FOR YOUR SKILLS AND ABILITIES

Gratitude is not always about other people. Have you stopped lately to think about your own unique talents and abilities and be thankful for them?

Feeling stuck? Unsure what your skills might be? Try asking those around you what they feel you do well. It can be as simple as being able to make a perfect cup of coffee, making sure that people feel cared for by always remembering birthdays, or offering newcomers a warm welcome.

Or perhaps you have skills that you take for granted but that others admire. Maybe in appreciating them you can then pass them on—for example, you might teach a child how to draw or paint, pass on your tech knowledge to an older member of your family, or show a friend how to do DIY.

THIS WEEK...

List three skills and abilities that you feel grateful for. You may like to include:

1. A note of why you appreciate these talents.

_____

_____

_____

_____

_____

_____

_____

2. An observation or compliment made by someone else that you can accept wholeheartedly.

_____

_____

_____

3. A deeper thought about your vision for your skills and talents in the future.

_____

_____

_____

REFLECT... ON YOUR SKILLS AND ABILITIES

MAKE TIME FOR FAMILY

Sometimes we are so busy being busy that we forget to let people know quite how grateful we are to have them in our lives. Relationships within families can be complicated, and may change over time. Even when we are fortunate enough to have strong bonds with our siblings, cousins, or parents, the chances are that we take our loved ones for granted much of the time.

One of the easiest ways to show gratitude, especially to parents and grandparents, is to offer them the gift of your time. That means time with full attention intact, and possibly a strong dose of patience, too—with both ears in action (especially if you are talking by phone). We are on this little planet for too short a spell not to make the most of the time we have together, even if the going gets tough and we fall out sometimes.

THIS WEEK...

Take the time to reflect on some or all of the following:

- Is there a relative whom you have not seen for some time? Is it time to give him or her a call to show your appreciation?
- How much of your life do you share with your parents and grandparents? Do you involve them to some extent, or are you living in a parallel universe?
- How much do you know about their lives? For example, do you know what went to school or whether they enjoyed sport?
- How often do you ask them to tell you about their past? How did they meet? What is their story?
- When you think back over your life, what have you learned from your parents, and what childhood moments do you feel grateful for?
- If there were troubled times, are you able to find ways to understand with appreciation and forgiveness in your heart?

REFLECT... ON HOW YOU CAN MAKE TIME FOR FAMILY

PRACTICE THOUGHT-SWAPPING

One way of coming to terms with living through a difficult time is to find a way of getting a new perspective on the experience. Reframing our thoughts is a subtle but powerful way of putting ourselves back into the driving seat of our own lives.

For example:

- If you find yourself thinking, "I am so fed up that X happened," try swapping it with, "At least I can be glad that Y didn't happen."
- "I am so fed up with having to chase my kids to get out of bed every morning" could become, "I am so glad that my kids are still young enough to need me— but it is time they learned to take personal responsibility for getting themselves up in the morning."
- "I wish people didn't come to me to offload all their problems" might become, "I hope I helped in some way, and it is good to know that I am trusted."
- Feeling that "I am so tired of having to go to the doctor for tests" is completely understandable, but it becomes easier to handle if it is reframed as, "I am glad to have these tests underway and am grateful that the doctor is taking them seriously."

THIS WEEK...

Catch your negative thoughts before they spiral and try to reframe them. Also listen out for the negative words you use to describe yourself or your situation. Reflect on how it benefits you and enhances your day to have more positive thoughts.

REFLECT... ON HAVING A MORE POSITIVE APPROACH TO THINGS

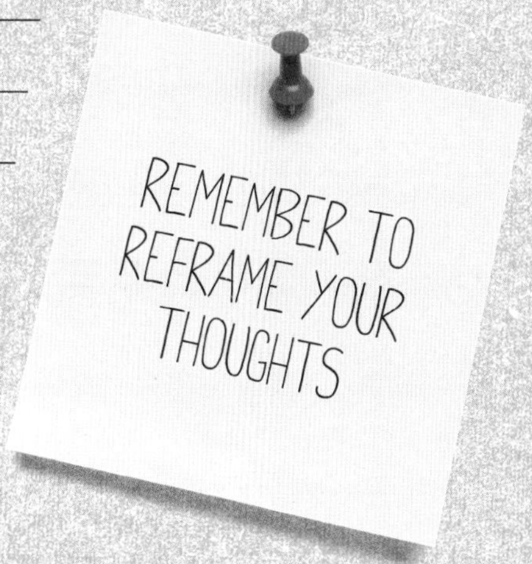

_____

_____

_____

_____

_____

_____

_____

_____

_____

_____

_____

_____

_____

_____

_____

_____

_____

REMEMBER TO REFRAME YOUR THOUGHTS

COMBAT CYNICISM

Sourness and cynicism have a way of crushing feel-good moments. Careworn thoughts of "What does he/she really want?" can take the edge off the pleasure of receiving an unplanned visit or enjoying a spontaneous gift. Becoming aware of how we use language when we talk to ourselves can be a surprisingly strong way to bring more gratitude and peace into our lives and relationships.

Receiving with negativity in our hearts means that we suffer pain from something that may have been given with genuine kindness. Not speaking up to say how we feel means that the person doesn't have the chance to realize the impact of their actions.

In her book *The Business Alchemist,* leadership coach Pilar Godino talks about each of us being motivated either to move toward or away from something in our conversation. Toward sentences are full of positivity and connection; away from sentences are negative and pull away from the risk of being hurt. For example:

- "My son only ever calls me when he wants something" is an away from sentence. The corresponding toward statement is "I have a good relationship with my son and I love it when he calls. He knows that I will say no if I cannot help for some reason."
- "My sister only gave me the furniture because she no longer has space for it" (away from), instead of, "She is a star for giving me first refusal" (toward).
- "If I hadn't called my friend she would not have invited me" (away from), instead of, "The party should be fun. I need to keep in touch better" (toward).

THIS WEEK...

Tune in to your internal chat and notice any "away from" statements you are telling yourself. These aren't "truth"—they are only your thoughts. How can you move toward something more positive?

REFLECT... ON HOW YOU CAN BECOME LESS CYNICAL AND MORE TRUSTING

REFLECT... ON THE PAST SIX MONTHS

Now we're halfway through the year, how do you feel so far? What experiences
have made you feel thankful? What impact has this had on your life?

_____

_____

_____

_____

_____

_____

_____

_____

_____

_____

_____

_____

_____

_____

_____

_____

_____

_____

_____

_____

BE THANKFUL FOR TIME OFF

All work and no play does nothing for your well-being— whether it's downtime at the weekend or a two-week vacation in the sun, honor and be grateful for your time off.

Taking time out from work and everyday life has a positive impact on our well-being. Studies show that, as well as being vital for stress relief, a change of pace can also boost creativity. Brain-imaging studies show that relaxation creates alpha waves in the brain that are key to being creative and thinking outside the box.

MAKE THE WEEKEND ABOUT YOU

Appreciating downtime doesn't necessarily mean spending lots of money. Winding down may be as simple as allocating yourself a duvet day, where you line up a box set to binge watch, or a stack of magazines you haven't had time to read, and unplug your digital devices for an afternoon. If your weekends are a whirl of chores, laundry, and life

admin, make a conscious decision to regularly switch off and put yourself back in balance. This might take some planning and effort—to ditch the to-do list every so often and make space to allow yourself to be idle.

CONNECT WITH FRIENDS

Alternatively, leisure activities with friends can re-energise and boost your well-being—plan a long walk in the great outdoors or a cozy pub lunch. Notice how taking even one day off from all work and responsibility can reset you mentally, and be thankful for the relaxation, fun, and laughter.

LIVE IN THE MOMENT

Whatever you opt for, try to be really present with what you're doing. Be aware of thought patterns if you start to drift into worrying about work or the week to come, and gently turn your attention back to the moment, allowing yourself to fully appreciate your time off.

THIS WEEK...

Once you've refueled your energy levels and creativity and truly appreciated some time off, set some good intentions to carry the boost into your week.

- Do a daily five-minute mindfulness exercise. Soon after you wake up, sit and breathe and really listen to your body, and consider what you're grateful for and ask what you need from your day.

- Build some mini time-out pockets into your day. For example, if you always eat at your desk take your lunch and eat it in a green space instead. Even 15 minutes can make a difference.

- If you commute, try to switch off work devices en route and get lost in a good book instead.

REFLECT... ON THE BENEFITS OF TAKING TIME OUT

SUCCESS AND GRATITUDE

It is very important to stop and take a moment to acknowledge life's milestones. How can we stride forward with clarity unless we know where we are in relation to where we began—and give thanks for getting to this point?

The following symbols of success and gratitude also represent important rites of passage:

Medals and trophies—Usually hard-won, they represent a moment when striving for personal goals and competing against the best deliver wonderful results, and they are received with gratitude. Olympians compete for the glory of winning, not for riches. They represent the appreciation and admiration of a nation. We, too, are usually more motivated by personal progress than by the material comforts that come in the wake of success.

Birthdays—Not always welcomed as we get older, they are nevertheless important. They are symbolic celebrations that represent rites of passage—each year of our life and the love, appreciation, and gratitude that others have for our presence on this earth. The gifts, cards, and tokens received and the way in which we celebrate help us to focus consciously on our gratitude for the past and present, as well as energizing our hopes and expectations for the future.

Examination results—of every sort. They represent the gratitude that you might choose to show to your teachers for taking you to this point, to your parents for supporting you, and to yourself for your achievements. If the grades are less than you had hoped for, there is reason to be grateful that you have more potential, and that the best is yet to come.

APPRECIATE YOUR UNSUNG HEROES

It's very easy to complain about those jobsworthy people who irritate us. But who are the people whose work you benefit from each day, who are rarely acknowledged for their dedication?

For example:

- The cleaner who focuses on the craftsmanship that went into making the sweep of the staircase that she dusts every day, instead of seeing her work as a chore.
- The nurse who has a waiting room full of patients, but still manages to greet every single person by name and with a smile, instead of focusing on the number of blood samples she has taken that day.
- The receptionist at the motel who speaks directly to your elderly mother and connects with her sense of humor, rather than judging her for her age and her wheelchair.
- The checkout boy who goes the extra mile to ensure you have some help with your groceries.
- The metro assistant who takes the time to show you a map rather than vaguely pointing you in the right direction.

Thinking about the people who touch your life indirectly helps to bring them into your consciousness when you are going about your daily tasks, so you are more likely to show appreciation or praise, and acknowledge them or mention them to other people. That is how gratitude grows and spreads.

THIS WEEK...

Take the time to really notice people at work in your community this week—those people who up to now you may have taken for granted—and treat them with the respect and thanks they deserve.

REFLECT... ON THE UNSUNG HEROES
WHO TOUCH YOUR LIFE

BE GRATEFUL AT WORK

Job satisfaction tends to evolve as much through the positive relationships we build in the workplace as from the work itself. Therefore relationships, rather than money, influence stability in the workforce.

Research suggests that those who feel appreciated by their boss, in particular, are less likely to be job-hunting. So it makes sense to do all you can to make your work environment a place driven by gratitude rather than blame, where people feel supported and appreciated rather than sidelined or overlooked.

Simple actions make a big difference, such as acknowledging colleagues as you pass them in the corridor, even if you don't have time to stop and chat. Those in more junior roles work hard but can be overlooked. And remember that senior colleagues may not be as confident as they appear. Saying thank you for the pay rise, the away-day, the staff party, or a well-run meeting can help to offer validation and oil the wheels of strong management. Easiest of all: when the going gets tough, smile and say something positive. It will make everyone feel better about the task in hand.

THIS WEEK...

- Banish the whinge culture. Moans and groans can drag everyone down—even if they are delivered with wit and humor. Try to find ways to evaluate and appreciate rather than denigrate.

- If someone shows you appreciation, keep those flowers or the card in plain sight. Symbols of gratitude can help others to raise their game, too, and the whole team to feel valued.

- Treat yourself to a plant, some flowers, or a picture for your desk.

- Make an effort to remember people's names—especially the names of those who are new to the organization. We all suffer from temporary amnesia from time to time, but knowing the names of those you work alongside is an important sign that you value their presence and contribution.

REFLECT... ON BEING MORE APPRECIATIVE AT WORK

BE THANKFUL FOR CHILDREN

We all love our children, but sometimes we need a reminder to take a step back
and be grateful for all that they bring to our lives.

There's a popular saying, modernized from a quote from the philosopher Epicurus:
"Remember when you wanted what you currently have." These few simple words can
be powerful enough to stop you in your tracks and bring about a jolt of appreciation
and gratitude for something you had maybe taken for granted—and for many of us,
our children will fall in to this category. Often children are longed for and planned for
long before they are conceived, and for some this longing will be stretched out for
months or years if fertility problems stand in the way.

However, parenting can be tough and exhausting, and in the daily whirl of nursery
and school runs and mess and sickness and lack of sleep, it can take us a moment to
stop and remember simply how lucky we are to have them.

One answer may be to take a leaf out of their books and learn to be more in the
moment. Kids are naturally good at this—they get lost in play and imagination and are
truly present in their lives—a quality that we tend to lose when we get older. Take a
minute to remember being a child and try to capture a little of how it felt to be fully
absorbed in a favorite activity—see if you can harness that feeling now.

TREASURE YOUR TIME

A few times each day, take a breath, remove distractions,
put your phone away, and set the intention to be
present with your children. Even if the prospect
of getting involved in the tenth game of trains
or schools isn't inviting when there's a pile of
laundry to do, follow their lead and appreciate
that they won't want to play these games
with you forever.

Another saying, "the days are long but the years are short", holds a lot of truth, even if it's hard to believe when you've been up since 4.30am. The years when kids are young fly by and there will come a time when you look back on this period with nostalgia and a full heart. So drink them in now—laugh at their laughter, smile at their sincerity, listen to their stories, snuggle in for bedtime books, take in their sweet scent, and hold their little bodies close. Take a mental snapshot of these moments to bring to mind in years to come.

Kids can find joy in the everyday and seeing the world afresh through their eyes can be a huge gift, if we're open to it. Rather than rushing them through the park to get to a destination, sometimes take pleasure in the journey with them and marvel at the "treasures," the leaves and conkers and sticks they collect on the way; ditch the chores sometimes and indulge in spontaneous games—blow raspberries and tickle little tummies and share silly jokes with older children.

GRATEFUL PARENTING

Robert Emmons, a professor at the University of California, has researched the benefits of gratitude and believes that it can strengthen relationships. We notice how someone is valuable to us and it creates a sense of appreciation that affects how we relate to them—so telling your child why you're grateful for them will encourage a more respectful and trusting bond.

One US study found that grateful parents were more likely to raise children who are happier and more appreciative of what they have and what others do for them. This happened through parents modeling gratitude themselves and also by them setting specific activities for kids, such as encouraging them to write thank-you letters.

Developing gratitude in childhood is thought to bring benefits in later life—studies have shown that people who are grateful are considerably happier and healthier. So encourage activities such as writing or drawing in a gratitude journal or getting into the habit of each family member stating something they're grateful for over dinner.

Parenting will always have its up and downs but cultivating gratitude in ourselves can help us to appreciate the everyday joys, and nurturing it in our children will boost their well-being, now and in the future.

REALLY BE THERE FOR LOVED ONES

Show your true appreciation for friends and family by being fully present when you're with them.

Many of us believe we are good listeners but to truly listen without judgment or an agenda, and with an open heart, is a skill that can be trickier than imagined. Research suggests that we only remember 25 to 50 percent of what we hear.

A good start to improving listening skills is to tune out distractions as much as possible (put that phone out of sight!) and give your undivided attention to what the other person is saying. To actively and accurately listen, use your body language to show you are hearing them (for example, plenty of eye contact and affirmative gestures such as nodding), and check you are hearing correctly by repeating back what you hear at intervals—even using some of the same words they have picked to show you are closely following what they're saying.

THIS WEEK...

Practice these listening skills:

- Try not to interrupt, and pause for a moment before responding, asking yourself, am I remaining with what they are telling me or coming in with my own agenda? Sticking with their agenda will also help you to listen empathically to what they are saying, which is likely to make them feel more heard and understood.

- Aim to step into their shoes for a while and think about what it must feel like to be them—by doing so you'll show compassion and willingness to go the extra mile in trying to understand.

REFLECT... ON THE BENEFITS OF LISTENING

BE GRATEFUL FOR DIFFERENCES

Appreciate differences and celebrate and be glad of diversity and all that
it brings to your life.

Whether consciously or not, we often choose friends who hold similar values and
beliefs to ourselves, who are from the same background or culture, and even those
who have similar levels of education. There's a popular saying, "friends are the family we
choose" and in our little friendship communities, it's common to have similar tastes in
music, books, or fashion, and to hold the same political or religious beliefs.

Yet if we can venture out of our comfort zones and be appreciative of those from
other cultures, or those who hold an alternative belief system to ours, it can enrich our
lives. A recent US study found that those who formed relationship with individuals
from different cultures experienced a boost to creativity and had enhanced cognitive
flexibility. Forming these relationships can help you see the world through a different
lens, and give a little insight into other ways of living.

Be grateful, too, for living in a society that permits freedom of speech and healthy
debate. Try to remain open to the views of others without feeling threatened and
become informed through reading different literature from different stances.

THIS WEEK...

Seek out different cultural experiences.

- Be open to culturally diverse friendships.
  Be aware of gravitating toward the same
  types of people and challenge yourself to
  make different alliances.
- Experiencing different countries
  undoubtedly broadens the mind—if you
  love to travel, plan your next vacation
  a little further afield and visit a country
  you've never been to, or one that has
  a religion that's unfamiliar.
- If you're a foodie, experiment with
  different cuisines. Seek out different
  restaurants in your area or simply find
  a recipe from a different region to try
  at home.

REFLECT... ON NOTICING DIFFERENCES

_____
_____
_____
_____
_____
_____
_____
_____
_____
_____
_____
_____
_____
_____
_____
_____
_____
_____
_____

REMEMBER:
CELEBRATE AND
APPRECIATE
DIFFERENCES

CHOOSE A HERO

Take a moment to appreciate your family, friends, neighbors, and colleagues—
honoring those who contribute to your world in the broadest sense:

- Who do you turn to during a time of turmoil?
- Who knows you better than you know yourself and loves you for who you are?
- Who tends to be there for you, no matter what?
- Who is your lifeline for the big stuff?
- Who keeps you sane with the little stuff?
- Who has made a difference to your life?
- Who has listened to your cares and worries without expecting anything in return?
- Who do you appreciate who does not always get shown appreciation?
- Who may be needing your support right now?
- Whom do you appreciate for the care they offer to others?
- Who would value you paying them greater attention,
  and cares when you are not around?

THIS WEEK...

Look at the questions above and take the time to properly reflect on them. Don't feel you have to answer them all at once.

Once you have your answers, think about how you can begin to show your gratitude to these special people.

REFLECT... ON THE HEROES IN YOUR LIFE

THINK OF SOMEONE

Sometimes in life we lose touch. Someone goes quiet. Often it is in the very moments that a friend, relative, or colleague seems to be most distant that he or she most needs your support and care.

I AM THINKING OF YOU

Have you ever received a gift or a gesture out of the blue? Do you remember how it made you feel? Unexpected gifts as gestures of kindness and support can be the most memorable, uplifting, and heartwarming of all.

A simple posy of flowers, a care parcel in the form of tea and cake, an invitation to lunch, a text message, or a phone call: there are numerous ways to reach out spontaneously to show our friends how much we care about them. Receiving a card unexpectedly from someone you haven't heard from for a long time can really make your day.

THIS WEEK...

Think about who needs you to share some goodwill with them today?

- Do you know someone who is going through a difficult time, who could do with an act of kindness or some moral support?

- Is there someone in your life who has been generous or supportive without expecting anything in return?

REFLECT... ON THOSE PEOPLE YOU'VE LOST TOUCH WITH RECENTLY

GRATITUDE THROUGH REMEMBRANCE

It can be cathartic to commit to paper all the things you appreciated about someone who is no longer so materially present in your life. It may help you to sense that they are still a part of your life in an important way, and to celebrate all that they meant to you.

I have learned four valuable things about grief:

- That when sadness wells up, be grateful for the tears and feel the sorrow deeply, so that the bright memories are etched all the more deeply into your heart.
- That "this too shall pass"—perhaps not today, or tomorrow, or next week, but in time something will shift so that we are left with gratitude, rather than pain.
- That laughter is cathartic. It has the power to change your mood instantly, and to increase the opportunity for joy. Sharing a simple joke can be just enough to remind you that it is okay to laugh, and that it is possible to be happy and to miss someone at the same time.
- To be patient—with yourself and others—and to accept that grief affects everyone differently, sometimes at unexpected times and in surprising ways.

THIS WEEK...

Think about a loved one you have lost and ask yourself the following questions

- How has this person helped to make me who I am today?
- How can I best give thanks for who they were and all they did?

- How can I make a contribution that honors them and offers grateful remembrance?
- Which places, what food, what music, what scents, what flowers remind me of them?

REFLECT... ON BEING GRATEFUL FOR SOMEONE YOU'VE LOST

_____

_____

_____

_____

_____

_____

_____

_____

_____

_____

_____

_____

_____

_____

_____

_____

_____

_____

GRATITUDE FOR GOOD HEALTH

When it comes to health, whether you're fighting fit or battling an illness,
it helps to count your blessings.

In a recent online poll in the US to find out what we feel most grateful for, health came out as a top contender, with 92 percent of us feeling most thankful for good health. And simply being in the habit of feeling gratitude can actually improve our health.

Robert Emmons, a professor at the University of California, explains that "Grateful people take better care of themselves and engage in more protective health behaviors like regular exercise, a healthy diet, and regular physical examinations." It's also thought that gratitude can have a stress-busting effect and improve the quality of sleep.

Remember what it's like when you're in the throes of a bad tummy bug or streaming cold and you can barely remember what it's like to feel healthy? The day you do feel better, you have a whole new appreciation for better health. Try to hold on

to that feeling with a little mindful reminder each morning of what feels good today and you'll avoid slipping into taking it for granted again.

WHEN YOU ARE ILL

This practice of daily gratitude can be effective even if you are sick or have health problems. Cultivating gratitude has been shown to help people deal with adversity. Try to be thankful for any part of you that is healthy, or anything in your day that felt physically good. It may be that you feel grateful for friends or family who are looking after you—perhaps they've taken time out of their lives to be with you or maybe they care for you with tenderness. Perhaps there's a feeling of closeness and connectedness that has resulted from their care.

"COUNT YOUR BLESSINGS
(INSTEAD OF SHEEP)."

Irving Berlin, (1888–1989), composer and lyricist

THIS WEEK...

If you are prone to taking your good health for granted, try counting your blessings by writing in a journal regularly—if you are short of time, it can be as quick and simple as having a notebook by your bed and jotting down a couple of health matters you're thankful for, whether it's having had a decent night's sleep or the pleasant sensation of walking home from work in the fresh air.

REFLECT... ON THE POSITIVE ASPECTS OF YOUR HEALTH

_____

_____

_____

_____

_____

_____

_____

_____

_____

_____

_____

_____

_____

_____

_____

_____

_____

_____

THE GRATITUDE TREE

Trees of all shapes and species are a wonderful symbol of the way that gratitude grows and envelops and nourishes us, providing the oxygen we need to thrive and survive.

The gratitude tree is sown from seeds of kindness and spreads via the roots of belonging. Gratitude grows like the solid trunk of an ancient oak, generating connectedness through its branches via the acts of giving, receiving, and reciprocating. As it matures over the seasons, the beautiful foliage of acceptance emerges, creating a canopy of ever-varying color and offering protection to all, and of course it bears the fruit of love, friendship, happiness, and forgiveness—that germinate further acts of kindness and spread the roots of gratitude further.

For the gratitude tree to thrive, there is an additional nutrient required in the earth that feeds the roots—and that is trust. Trust that the gifts are bestowed with no artificial additive of expectation; and that the tree will be nurtured with goodwill and watered with appreciation—to protect it from neglect or drought.

FOCUS ON HAVING ENOUGH

Contentment is defined as a state of happiness and peaceful satisfaction. Seeking contentment is about having "enough." We feel grateful for what we have without hungering for more.

Instead of a sense of entitlement, a kind of faith develops that we will be provided for. Sometimes having enough and feeling contented can mean living modestly—but at its heart it is more about trust, about believing that there is "more than enough to go round."

Why, then, when we have so much to be grateful for, do we spend so much time complaining, regretting, or wishing? The clue may lie in our sense of entitlement. It leaves us wanting, expecting, and disappointed, by contrast with having enough, which guides us to a place of gratitude and trust.

Can it be that in modern times, when so many of us live in relative comfort (compared to previous generations), we have come to expect certain things as our right? When these are lacking, we feel that we have been deprived in some way, rather than noticing all that we have and appreciating the gift. A sense of entitlement provides very little space for gratitude to flourish because it is self-orientated. There is no giving and receiving, there is only taking. We lack balance.

In a culture of acquisition we will always feel that we are entitled to more (bigger bonuses, greater bandwidth, faster cars, more exotic vacations), and that we can never have enough. Ultimately this lack of exchange can lead to loneliness and a feeling of being separate from the rest of the world. In a very real sense, our cultural sense of entitlement is upsetting the balance of the entire natural world.

THE DANGER OF ENTITLEMENT

Much of the discontent and unhappiness we feel in life is connected to the things we do not have. When we compare our own situation with other people's we will always be left wanting—not least because we don't know the full picture. We don't really know what anyone else's life is actually like.

However, the magic is that disappointment and dissatisfaction are not always negative; they can also become a driving force that leads us to strive and to achieve. By taking stock when we feel negative, we can choose to focus on gratitude by feeling thankful for future possibilities instead. Once we acknowledge that we have choice in our lives, we also realize that we can bring about change. For example, not earning enough to buy the house of your dreams might lead you to come up with a strategy for co-purchase or to choose to rent somewhere beautiful instead. Being unhappy in a relationship may lead to a re-evaluation of your actions and choices—and the decision to try to work on things together rather than apportion blame or walk away.

When we expect less and appreciate more, something interesting happens: levels of satisfaction about small things become higher. The child who has strived to improve on a D grade is thrilled with their C and starts to see a B as possible; the person who earns very little appreciates every penny of a performance bonus and has faith in their prospects for the future. Letting go of the idea that we are entitled and swapping it for a feeling of appreciation is a powerful step toward inner contentment and happiness.

THIS WEEK...

Think about an area of life about which you often have negative thoughts. Explore why it is you feel you deserve more or better in this area. How can you see what you do have in a more positive way?

REFLECT... ON HAVING ENOUGH

_____
_____
_____
_____
_____
_____
_____
_____
_____
_____
_____
_____
_____
_____
_____
_____
_____
_____
_____
_____
_____
_____

COMPASSION IN ACTION

Heinrich Steinmeyer, a German soldier, was captured in France at the age
of 19 during the Second World War. He was removed to Cultybraggan,
a prisoner-of-war camp near to Comrie village in Perthshire, Scotland, and
stayed there from November 1944 until June 1945. He was relocated twice
before being released in 1948.

A young man from a poor background, Steinmeyer was enrolled in the Hitler Youth
and was a member of the notorious Waffen SS at the time of his capture. He would
have considered the British people his enemy.

However, much to his surprise, he found himself in the heart of a community that
had the grace to treat him with kindness. He was befriended by local schoolchildren
who got chatting to him through the fence of the prison, one of whom eventually
became his wife. He stayed on in Scotland after the war, developing firm friendships
with those he had come to know.

His story hit the news headlines because following his death at the age of 90, it was
revealed that Steinmeyer had left his savings of £384,000 to "the elderly" in the village
in Perthshire where he had been held prisoner.

His will stated: "Herewith, I would like to express my gratitude to the people of
Scotland for the kindness and generosity that I have experienced in Scotland during my
imprisonment of war and hereafter."

BE GRATEFUL FOR FRIENDS

One area where we are rarely left wanting is in the field of friendship. As the saying goes, "friends are the family that we choose for ourselves." Showing conscious appreciation is a vital part of building and maintaining friendships and becomes increasingly important as we get older.

We know we are blessed with the friends whom we invite into our life—they make us laugh, they comfort and support us through the tough times, they remind us of who we are and what life is all about. Finding ways to offer thanks to those we hold most dear is a joy and a privilege, and we must do it as often and as much as possible!

Showing gratitude and appreciation for our closest friends tends to be one of the easiest things in the world. We know how they think, what they like, what makes them laugh—and what they would most appreciate. The person whom you turn toward to talk through your woes is not always the same person you choose to go partying with, although you probably appreciate them equally.

RESPECTING FRIENDS

We tend to be more relaxed and able to be ourselves with our friends than with our family. Even so, it is possible to take someone we care about for granted, inadvertently.

- When you think of your friendship circle, do some people get the fun assignments while others get the angst?
- When you get in touch, do you respect their time? Or do you expect them to "drop everything" and be there for you?

SPECIAL MEMORIES

There is a truism that each moment of life is lived forward but tends to be understood backward. When we think back to times past, we may have favorite memories—of precious moments, of places we have seen, experiences we have had, our successes, our losses, and, as we get older, perhaps sharing our life with someone special, marriage, or the birth of children or grandchildren. We savor fond recollections of friendship and companionship, and are more likely to appreciate what has gone before—and to view misunderstandings with compassion and increased perspective.

THIS WEEK...

Take a moment to honor and focus on your friends.

- Think about them one at a time—what they look like, how they smile and laugh, a key moment that you have shared together.
- If you were to move home or leave school/college/your job tomorrow, who would you want to contact to thank for the part they played in your life?
- Who would you like to leave a "legacy letter" for—to offer gratitude and encouragement for their future?

REFLECT... ON SPECIAL FRIENDSHIPS

EXPERIENCING FREEDOM

Robin, 44, is a recovering cancer patient. "Extreme suffering becomes in the end a form of liberation. When you have nothing left to lose, you no longer care what anyone thinks. When you no longer fear death, you are free to live the better life that you always wanted."

He and his family have found a new sense of gratitude in the simple joy of being in each other's company. "The little things no longer irritate," says Robin's wife. "Every day feels more precious now."

"WEAR GRATITUDE LIKE A CLOAK AND IT WILL SUSTAIN EVERY CORNER OF YOUR LIFE."

Rumi (1207–1273), poet and mystic

GRATITUDE FOR WHO YOU ARE RIGHT NOW

How can we better appreciate who we are in order to transform ourselves into what we can become? Can discontent or disappointment about something in your past be transformed into acceptance, or recharged in a way that helps you to let go and move forward? The science of happiness and research into gratitude suggest that it can.

Scientists tell us that it is impossible to feel genuinely positive about something at the same time as feeling negative. We can transform our negative feelings by accepting that they exist and choosing to overlay them with a new and more positive outlook. Nurturing thankfulness for all that we have can be re-energizing and enough to drive us forward with creative change. It is forgiveness in action.

* Take a moment to give thanks for the way you see the world: your senses, your thoughts, your choices, your actions.
* Allow yourself to appreciate all the qualities you have—and those you would like to enhance and improve.
* Think back over your life and think of three things that you are proud of.
* Think of one thing that you feel regretful or unhappy about.
* Consider your future and one thing you would value doing more of. Can you put in place a plan or steps to make that happen?

THIS WEEK...

Using the pointers above, try writing yourself a thank-you message or letter. Remember, there are no negative statements allowed and this is for your eyes only. Reflect on the feelings that come up for you as you do this.

REFLECT... ON BEING KIND TO YOURSELF

PAY IT FORWARD

Feeling gratitude for our work and the pathway to learning helps us to become aware of where we are on the bigger path. Those who live life with a generous heart learn that if we give to others with no expectation of receiving in return, we are more likely to receive unexpected trust, loyalty, and other heartfelt benefits.

The business coach Bev James has embraced this philosophy throughout her career. She has offered sound advice freely, given away information on her website at no cost, and looked after her loved ones and colleagues generously. Over time her business has grown and expanded. She makes no distinction between her well-known clients and those who have slowly furrowed their own path. She pays it forward and has found that those she has helped have always willingly given back in exchange. Consider:

- When someone asks you for a favor, how do you feel?
- Do you offer your time and knowledge willingly, with good heart?
- Is there someone you could help today with no expectation of reward?
- Has someone offered you support, help, or guidance at some time, simply out of the kindness of their heart?

Taking time to offer them thanks, whether actually or in your heart—or on paper—will help to cement the feeling of contentment and connectedness. When we appreciate that we are all part of the same whole, we see very clearly that giving to others is exactly the same as giving to ourselves.

THIS WEEK...

Think about a good deed someone has done you in the past and how it made you feel. Reflect on small ways you can pay it forward by offering something of yourself without expecting anything in return.

REFLECT... ON PAYING IT FORWARD

_____
_____
_____
_____
_____
_____
_____
_____
_____
_____
_____
_____
_____
_____
_____
_____
_____
_____

WORK OUT YOUR LEGACY

It is natural to want to be remembered warmly and with gratitude when we leave school, a place of work, a neighborhood—and ultimately this earth. Most people, as they get older, give some thought to their legacy. However, sometimes we become so focused on the destination that we forget to be thankful for what we have learned along the way.

Modesty is an admirable trait, but not when it diminishes life and makes everything invisible. Looking toward the future with gratitude and focused intention helps us to make our lives feel more worthwhile in the present moment.

- What can you be grateful for that you would like others to share in and to benefit from?
- What are the "lessons in life" that you would like to share so that others have the chance to see life through your eyes?
- Where have you traveled and what have you seen that might fascinate and interest future generations?
- What mistakes have you made that you are grateful for because you have learned from them, and that others might learn from too?
- Which people in your life have had a positive impact on you, whose memory you would like to keep alive?

THIS WEEK...

Look back through photographs across the years, perhaps including family and friends in your musings. What memories and lessons does doing this spark in you? Who would you like to share these with so that they can benefit the next generation, too?

REFLECT... ON WHAT YOUR LEGACY WILL BE

LIGHT A CANDLE

Has someone you cared about died recently? Have you parted from someone you care about? Perhaps you have been separated temporarily by work or geographical distance? Lighting a candle in remembrance or as a tribute is a very simple symbol of gratitude for the light and energy that others bring to our life.

A single candle can shine a light that is brighter than its flame, with an intensity that matches the strongest and most sincere of feelings.

Meditating on a single flame is a powerful way to concentrate our innermost thoughts. It helps us to enter a frame of mind in which we feel able to offer thanks for all that is sacred, to be grateful for the continued well-being of our loved ones, or to make sense of our feelings and our memories.

THIS WEEK...

Light your candle in silence, and take a moment to focus peacefully and completely on the person you are thinking of. If you are able to play some music that reflects your mood, the intensity will be increased as more of your senses will be involved in the tribute. Breathe slowly and consciously, while saying or thinking whatever comes to mind in farewell, sorrow, appreciation, or remembrance.

REFLECT... ON SOMEONE SPECIAL

FIND A GRATITUDE CHALLENGE

This one needs time to think about and plan. Many people who have taken up a large-scale challenge have done so because they want to give back in some way —show their thanks—or offer support. We probably all know people who have taken action to walk, run, swim, climb, or skydive, or who have undertaken some other tremendous feat for the benefit of a cause.

Choosing a challenge for the good of others has the benefit of helping other people to get the "feel-good factor" by helping you, sponsoring you, and sharing in the glory of your success. The impact can be personally transformative, too. Here are some words from those who set themselves a challenge:

- "I climbed Mount Kilimanjaro to celebrate my 60th birthday and to test my resilience, while also raising money for my local hospital. On the trip I also happened to meet the man who would become my husband, which was a joy-filled bonus!" *Vanda*

- "I wanted to challenge myself by running a half-marathon and it was the perfect way to raise funds for the hospice that cared for our family friend, Aunty Margaret, too. The training was tough, but I loved taking part in the event and am ready to train for my next event now!" *Libby*

THIS WEEK...

Think about whether there is something you could undertake for a good cause? Is there an organization that you'd like to thank, someone you'd like to remember? Try sitting with the idea for a little while. You will know when it is right for you to take action.

REFLECT... ON FINDING A GRATITUDE CHALLENGE

FIND GRATITUDE BY MAKING AMENDS

Most families and friends experience misunderstandings from time to time, but sometimes these transform into full-blown estrangement. Making amends requires someone to make a positive choice—to risk a moment of rejection by putting another person's needs before their own.

The chances are that once you have reached out, even if there is a period of unsettled adjustment, there will be a reciprocal sense of gratitude that you have been in contact and that a bridge has been built. If someone has upset you, try putting yourself in their shoes for a moment. Does it alter your perspective? Can you try to see the world through a new lens and let go of the negativity? When we hold on to irritation with someone, ultimately we are often causing more disruption to ourselves than to them.

Has your own behavior caused you a problem that you find it hard to forgive yourself for? When we hold on to negative feelings, they hurt us more than they hurt the person or event that we feel negative about. By digging deep and finding a way to accept your feelings, it becomes possible to start to transform them into something more constructive. Accepting the past and offering forgiveness either actually or privately, in your own heart, is an important step toward living life with gratitude—for the understanding of what has been and the awareness that it offers. In time we can learn to forgive, and to feel grateful for the greater understanding we have developed.

THIS WEEK...

Think about someone you could reach out to and make amends. Or ask yourself if you're holding on to anger and resentment about a past hurt. Try writing a letter to that person; even if you don't send it, the act of writing it will be helpful to you.

REFLECT... ON MAKING AMENDS

EMBRACE YOUR ROLE AS CARER

For many, the role of father, mother, home-maker, provider, or carer—in whatever form that takes—is not only a personal role, it becomes their main reason for being, and a purpose for life. Sometimes as a carer we don't receive gratitude and that can be challenging.

Caring for others is a vital part of many people's professions. Nurses, care workers, teachers, and social workers have all chosen professions where the needs of others are the central focal point of every day. Happiness comes, not necessarily from the task, which can be demanding and sometimes exhausting, but from the sense of purpose, the sense of belonging, and the gratitude that is bestowed in return.

Caring for others delivers gratitude in the short term and happiness in the long term. It may take a child their entire lifetime to realize how tenderly they were cared for; an elderly person may be too encumbered by pain to recognize who is looking after them, until the pain subsides; a teacher may never get the thanks he deserves, but may gain satisfaction from students' positive exam results, or from noticing that someone they once taught has risen to professional success.

THIS WEEK...

Assess your altruism:

- How easy do you find it to put the needs of others before your own? How happy does it make you feel?
- When is the last time you cared for someone, without expecting thanks in return. Did the feeling of well-being outweigh your wish for gratitude?
- Think of three things, however large or small, that you could do for someone today. Write them down, and pledge with a happy heart to do as you say.

REFLECT... ON HOW YOU CARE FOR PEOPLE

BE THANKFUL FOR OPPORTUNITIES TO LEARN

Many of us are in the privileged position of having the opportunity to learn new things—whether it's taking up lessons in something or simply using the internet or the library as a source of learning. Take time to be grateful for and maximize the opportunity. Let go of any preconceptions about what your skills and talents might be and open your mind to new experiences and opportunities.

Ken Robinson, British author, speaker, and international advisor on education, is passionate about the importance of creativity in our education systems and in our personal development. He has a heartfelt belief that we each have unique talents and abilities that can inspire us to achieve much more than we currently dream possible. But in order to find out what those talents are, we need to tune into the world of our imagination, our intuition, and our senses, to truly experience and be stimulated by the world. He calls the process of loving what you do and doing what you love being "in your element."

DON'T BE OLD BEFORE YOUR TIME

Avoid the mindset that you're too old to learn something new or realize your dreams and be grateful for the opportunity. Getting older can be a time of liberation, laughter, and fun. Look forward to your future. When you look back, what will you respect about the choices you have made? And what will you regret that you haven't done? Honor your life by seizing your opportunities.

When you make your decisions, don't let age be the excuse that got in your way. Many people begin to live their lives more safely as they get older. Understandably, they feel more physically vulnerable or less energetic. But there are examples all around the world of healthy people in their nineties undertaking brave endeavors, just as there are people in their forties who have already said goodbye to their youth. Have you got a dream that you put to one side when you were younger?

THIS WEEK...

Bring your dreams to life. When is the last time you learned something new? Make this the week you start turning your dreams into reality. Learning new skills and acquiring knowledge boosts confidence and makes us happier.

- Write down things you've always dreamed of doing—don't feel restricted or think of barriers. Just write what's in your heart. For example, have you ever dreamed of learning to skydive, dance, ride a horse or a motorcycle? Have you had a hankering to learn a language, paint, take up carpentry, or even start a business?

- Now think about what excuses you have been putting in your way. Do you want to look back in years to come and regret that you never tried? Or are you willing to take a risk and stretch your boundaries for the sake of curiosity and the risk of happiness?

- Finally, write down your first action toward achieving your goal. It may be research or it may be seeking advice or telling a friend. When you have done that action, write down your next action, and so on.

Week 45

REFLECT... ON BEING THANKFUL FOR OPPORTUNITIES TO LEARN

GRATITUDE GURU: DAVID STEINDL-RAST

No book on gratitude is complete without mentioning David Steindl-Rast OSB, an Austrian-born Catholic Benedictine monk with a peaceful and mesmeric voice, who cofounded a center for spiritual studies in 1968 with teachers from the Buddhist, Sufi , Hindu, and Jewish faiths. Brother David also cofounded the nonprofit A Network for Grateful Living, which is dedicated to gratefulness as a route to transformation in all societies. His videos and talks are an inspirational joy for everyone who is on a mission to live life more thankfully (see Resources, page 189).

"STOP. LOOK. GO. THAT'S ALL."

David Steindl-Rast (1926–)

CELEBRATE YOUR LIFE

When one of my closest friends celebrated a milestone birthday, she decided to invite all her friends from every stage of her life to celebrate. Looking around the room, it was like seeing a picture of different stages of her life in microcosm.

A few months later she was diagnosed with a brain tumor, and she faced that terrifying time with her characteristic positivity and bravery. Fortunately, she has recovered fully, but looking back on the ups and downs of her life—and her year—she commented, "I was so happy at my party. I looked around the room at all the friends who were there, and I thought to myself, 'It has all been all right. I have done a good job. My life has been worthwhile. I love my family; my husband and I are still enjoying life together; my children are well balanced and happy, and soon to be embarking on their own lives; and I am surrounded by friends whom I love and who have witnessed my life with all its ups and downs. I have been so lucky, and I am so happy with my life'."

What I loved and respected about her words was her ability to notice and appreciate the importance of that moment. She saw that all the actions and decisions she had taken over the course of her life had led to that moment of recognition and celebration. She hadn't arranged the party as a review of her life; she arranged it to have fun and enjoy the company of friends, and to celebrate a mid-life coming of age. But in taking the time to reflect on that shared moment with other people, she realized how happy she was and that realization help her to embrace the next phase of life, too.

THIS WEEK...

Reflect on every stage of your life through the decades you've lived so far. What were the key moments? Who were the key people?

What were the most positive things that happened to you?

REFLECT... ON YOUR LIFE SO FAR

BE THANKFUL FOR NATURE

There are so many benefits to taking time to tune into and be grateful for the great outdoors. Spending time in nature is one of the most powerful anti-depressants available to us—it's free and provides an easy route to a happier life. Breathing sea air, trekking through a forest, walking along a riverbank, or simply visiting a park are all ways to get close to nature. City dwellers will of course need to make more effort to get a nature fix, but it's a journey worth making.

Humans weren't meant to live in confined air-conditioned or centrally heated places. It's unnatural and unhealthy to stay indoors for long periods of time but increasingly children, especially, are tied to activities that limit the amount of time they spend outside. This makes them more likely to gain weight and causes them to be deficient in Vitamin D due to a lack of exposure to sunlight.

Scientists in Japan monitored the effects of a practice known as Shinrin-yoku, which means forest-bathing. Half of the participants were sent into a forest, and the other half into a city. The next day, they swapped places. Those who returned from the forest were found to have "lower concentrations of cortisol, lower pulse rate, and lower blood pressure." There is also evidence that chemicals emitted by plants, known as phytoncides, help to strengthen immunity.

THIS WEEK...

Plan a nature discovery weekend and take the time to be grateful for your surroundings:

- Check your local area for green spaces and plan a visit.
- Slowing down and walking quietly will allow you to become fully mindful and to notice plants and wildlife.

- Turn off your phone—you don't need to announce your nature trip on social media. Just live in the moment.
- Reflect on what in your surroundings you were grateful for and how being close to nature made you feel.

REFLECT... ON ALL THE NATURE AROUND YOU

APPRECIATE THE FUNNY SIDE OF LIFE

Do you remember what it feels like to be overcome with giggles or shake with uncontrollable laughter so that it was impossible to speak? To feel consumed by the joy of a single moment, shared with someone you care about or can have fun with? It probably happened frequently when you were growing up, but as we get older it becomes less common for us to let go and have a really good laugh.

Laughter wipes away tension in a single breath and turns a frowning face into one that is alive and beautiful. It doesn't take much to trigger a giggle: just thinking about something funny that has happened can provoke laughter and increase happiness. When we are tense, we become very serious—but turning things around in your mind can be a great way to change your mood and appreciate the lighter side of life.

- Check your laughter meter. When is the last time you had a really great laugh? Do you know what makes you laugh?
- When was the last time you laughed at yourself? When was the last time someone else had a laugh at your expense, without you taking it personally? Is there a chance you take yourself too seriously? Do you need to lighten up a bit in order to enjoy life?

THIS WEEK...

Find something to laugh about every day if you can.

- Most of us know someone who makes us laugh and with whom we can really let our hair down. Make time to meet up with or connect with him or her. Recalling old times and chuckling about new ones is a wonderful shortcut to happiness.

- Consider treating yourself to a self-styled comedy night. Hire the funniest movie you can find and allow yourself to remember what it feels like to laugh just for the sake of it.
- Tell someone a silly joke, read a favorite cartoon strip, look for the absurd in every situation.

REFLECT... ON HOW IT FELT TO HAVE FUN

APPRECIATE THE PRESENT MOMENT

Paying attention to the present moment—being mindful—encourages careful observation and appreciation of the things around us. Living life consciously puts more emphasis on the present moment. It brings our present actions into clear focus; encourages us to mind what we think and to think about what we do and say.

Practising mindfulness puts us in closer touch with our feelings, our reactions, and our intuition, because there are no distractions. By appreciating the present, we can also choose to be happy with this moment—and recognize with every second, every minute, and every hour that passes that we are right here, right now, and can influence the future—in any way we choose.

AWAKEN YOUR SENSES

Your senses send messages to the brain. When your senses are alert, you feel more alive. Focus fully on what you are doing at every moment of the day. There is joy to be had in every task: the sight of a robin hopping about while you are weeding; the smell of the ingredients while you are baking; the sound of your children chattering while discovering their world; the hug or touch of a friend or lover. Appreciating the small things awakens awareness of the bigger things, and helps to put us back in touch with our true selves.

THE BENEFITS

By being more present—more mindful of the present moment—we can learn to let go of the need to control our experiences. We can become more compassionate toward ourselves and more accepting of how things are. It is not about trying to stop things or change them and this acceptance can, in itself, make us more relaxed, calm, and happy. Some will find it possible to get more pleasure and happiness out of everyday chores by tuning into them and focusing on the positive experience, instead of dreading them and just wishing they were over. So, yes, you really can be happy doing the vacuuming!

THIS WEEK...

Try either or both of these meditations to help you stay relaxed and present. Allow any thoughts that come into your mind—they're quite normal—and just gradually bring your attention back to your breath. Don't criticize or judge your wandering mind.

- Make sure that both feet are firmly on the ground and move your attention to the soles of your feet. Imagine that you are breathing in and out through the soles of your feet. Continue for a few breaths or for as long as you wish.

- Sitting or lying in a relaxed position, focus on your breathing and notice where you feel the breath most strongly—for example, in your chest or lower down in your belly. Notice the sensations of breathing. You may want to place a hand on your chest or belly. As you watch your breath, stay with the length of the in-breath—follow it through. Then do the same with the out-breath. Do this for as long and as often as you wish.

REFLECT... ON BEING MORE MINDFUL

_____

_____

_____

_____

_____

_____

_____

_____

_____

_____

_____

_____

_____

_____

_____

_____

_____

_____

_____

_____

_____

_____

_____

GRATITUDE GURU: MARTIN SELIGMAN

The internationally renowned psychologist Professor Martin Seligman is director of the Penn Positive Psychology Center at Pennsylvania State University. Commonly referred to as the founder of the concept of positive psychology, he has spent his career researching the factors that contribute to pessimism or optimism in outlook, and whether these characteristics are innate or learned.

Professor Seligman has devised a series of measures that help to prove that those with a "can do" attitude, who believe that they have control over their life, and who understand that they can choose how to respond to adversity or obstacles, tend to be in better physical health and more resilient. They may even live longer. Pessimists, on the other hand, who don't believe that anything they do will change their circumstances, are triggering activity in the brain that encourages "learned helplessness." The findings tend to show that they are less resistant when illness strikes, and may even die younger than those who show optimism. Optimistic people are not necessarily more grateful than pessimists. However, research is showing that practicing gratitude may be the key to enabling pessimists to become more optimistic.

"I DON'T THINK YOU CAN HAVE A POSITIVE FUTURE
UNLESS YOU CAN ENVISION ONE."

Martin Seligman (1942–)

GIVE YOUR TIME OR MONEY

Giving money, possessions, or even your time to others is perhaps the ultimate way to show thanks. The good news is that it's beneficial for you. It will make you happy and make you feel better about yourself.

I spoke recently to someone whose mother had moved to a smaller home. Sorting through all her possessions and deciding what to let go had been painful for both of them. Even passing books and goods on to a thrift store had proved a hard adjustment. But the charity they chose runs a scheme whereby donors are sent an update on how much money their items have raised. Receiving these letters made my friend's mother so happy that over time she began to give away even more.

In 2010, the Charities Aid Foundation (CAF) joined with *The Sunday Times* to ask 69 of the UK's wealthiest people about the reasons for their philanthropy. The majority said the main reason was that they enjoyed giving. Over half wanted to leave a positive legacy. In the United States, Bill Gates is leading the way via the Bill and Melinda Gates Foundation. He has personally donated millions of dollars and, with Warren Buffett, has launched "The Giving Pledge," inviting billionaires to make a moral pledge to leave at least 50 percent of their fortunes as a legacy to philanthropic causes. Media mogul Simon Cowell has been quoted in the past as crediting Oprah Winfrey for helping him to discover how surprisingly good it feels to give money away.

SERVING OTHERS

But giving isn't just about money. The most valuable gift of all is your personal time—time spent in the service of others, listening and paying attention. The concept of service may seem old-fashioned in the modern world, but the nature of service goes much deeper than the odd good deed. When we are able to serve others, modestly, but putting the needs of the ego to one side, we become more humble, less focused on self, and more aware of the strengths of those around us.

We can also give by simply being kind to others. Studies have proven again and again that the quickest and most satisfying route to finding happiness is not to think about yourself all the time, but instead to focus on other people and what they need. As human beings we are social creatures who like to be connected to one another. Giving and gratitude are essential ingredients in the formulation and experience of happiness.

THIS WEEK...

Try taking the Good Deed Pledge. It may turn out to be the best good deed you have ever done for yourself!

- Consider pledging to yourself and others today that you will consciously do one good deed per day, no matter how small, for the next ten days; and that, at the end of those ten days, you will repeat the pledge.
- Make a list of deeds done and ask yourself whether or not each one made you happy.

REFLECT... ON GIVING YOUR TIME OR MONEY

_____

_____

_____

_____

_____

_____

_____

_____

_____

_____

_____

_____

_____

_____

_____

_____

_____

_____

_____

_____

BIRTHDAY GIFTS THAT GIVE

Birthdays are a wonderful time to show our appreciation. They have been celebrated with gifts at least since the time of the pharaohs in Ancient Egypt, when astrologers needed to know details of date and time of birth in order to cast a horoscope for the leaders of the day, who were granted god-like status. Sharing the occasion of your birthday with others, and having them share theirs with you, is a wonderful way to celebrate each new age, as well as honoring life's transitions and rites of passage.

- The next time you have a birthday to celebrate, consider giving gifts to others instead of waiting to receive them!
- Instead of giving gifts to each other, consider giving time or money to a humanitarian cause or a welfare organization.
- Pass on a gift that has had meaning for you in the past: perhaps you were given piece of jewelry, a book, a pen, or an ornament for a significant birthday, which you love but no longer use. Do you know someone who is the same age as you were then who would enjoy it?

CELEBRATING GOOD TIMES AND GREAT MEMORIES

We are so fortunate to be living in an age where it is possible to share photos, stories, and memories so widely and so quickly. Here are some ideas people shared:

- "I create a photographic calendar each year as a Christmas present for the family, which records key moments of the year (and includes everyone's birthdays, too!). The grandparents really appreciate it and always look forward to it." *Sue*
- "For my daughter's 21st birthday I created a photo record of her life with captions and stories. She loved it and was so grateful as it reminded her of her early days." *Nicole*
- "My father was a very talented artist, though very modest about his skills. I decided to have a number of his pictures turned into cards. We have had so much positive feedback that I am going to create some more." *Phil*

GIVE THANKS WITH A HUG

This is perhaps the simplest way to show thanks to someone, and the good news
is that there are plenty of benefits for you too!

Scientists tell us that the roots of self-esteem stem from the earliest stages of our life.
According to Sue Gerhardt, author of *Why Love Matters*, the unconditional love that we
receive as babies appears to influence brain development. Babies who are comforted
when they cry learn to soothe themselves as they grow, whereas babies who are left
to cry develop a highly sensitized response to stress, which means that they find it
harder to manage stress when they are adults.

But why is this? When we are stressed or feel in danger, the body produces a
hormone called cortisol. We need a certain amount of cortisol, but in high stress
situations, we produce too much, too often, which can have a tiring effect on the body
and leave people less able to manage their emotions. Those who are highly sensitive
to stress will try to self-soothe—for example, by eating high-carbohydrate foods.
The good news is that getting physical with someone else will reduce your stress
levels, reduce your cortisol levels, and increase the production of oxytocin, a "happy"
hormone, in the body. All of this will make you feel happier, and will also boost
your immune system. It will also have huge benefits for the person you're showing
gratitude to.

THIS WEEK...

Rather than just saying thanks, show your
gratitude to someone by giving them a hug.
Also look out for family or friends who might
be going through a difficult time. Making the
effort to meet up with them so that you can
give them a much-needed a hug might just
turn things around for them in a way that
a sympathetic text message or email won't.

REFLECT... ON GIVING THANKS WITH A HUG

_____

_____

_____

_____

_____

_____

_____

_____

_____

_____

_____

_____

_____

_____

_____

_____

_____

_____

REFLECT ON YOUR YEAR

In reaching the final weekly activity, I truly hope the ideas and action points have inspired you to arrive at a place where showing thanks is easier and brings you happiness and many rewards.

Flick back through the book, over the full 52 weeks, and use the checklist on pages 186–187 to work out those activities that suited you best and were most effective. Read back over your reflections and work out what, if anything, you might do differently. There are pages at the back of the book if you want to reflect further on what you have learnt.

If you'd like to continue living a more grateful life, you might want to start a gratitude journal. Turn to pages 174–177 for guidance on doing this.

THIS WEEK...

Write a pledge to continue showing your thanks whenever you can and to pass on this positive trait to others. Think about who in your life might benefit from having a more positive and grateful attitude, and how might you go about sharing what you've learnt?

52+53
Dec 21-27
Dec 28 - Jan 3

REFLECT... ON A YEAR OF LIVING THANKFULLY

REFLECT... ON A YEAR OF LIVING THANKFULLY

"PRESERVE YOUR MEMORIES, KEEP THEM WELL."

Louisa May Alcott (1832–1888), writer

A GRATITUDE JOURNAL

An attitude of gratitude gains strength the more we practice it, so on these pages I'm going to share with you ways of continuing to focus and reflect on ways to be thankful with a carefully chosen gift to yourself: your gratitude journal, app, or diary.

Give your choice of journal some thought before you embark on your mission of gratitude, because it needs to become a joy to use. I was very lucky that a dear friend had given me a beautiful notebook that had been waiting two years for the right moment to be used. It was exactly the right size, shape, and quality to inspire me— but I am an old-fashioned pen-and-paper person. If you are likely to share some key moments on Twitter or Pinterest, you may prefer to use your phone or a specially designed app to record your moments of gratitude.

Do remember that your journal is intended for you personally, rather than your community of friends, as some comments may be quite private. You may wish to be selective about what you share more broadly so that you don't find yourself restraining your thoughts in your daily journal for fear of what others will think.

BEGINNING YOUR JOURNAL

As you complete your journal, it will become a resource to treasure, that will reflect your thoughts and your progress back to you over time. There are many books and resources on journaling, and the pages that follow include a few guidelines that will help you to decide when and how keeping a journal will work for you.

First a little note of what your journal is not: it is not a shopping list, nor a "to do" list, nor a diary of events. It is, however, a place where you can express yourself freely and reflect not only on the things you feel grateful for, but also on ways you can turn negative reactions into something more positive. Over time, it will become a dossier of appreciation, a cluster of precious moments that connect you to the people in your life, to the world, and all the good things in it.

Getting started is the easy bit: keeping going can be tougher. If completing the journal every day becomes a chore, and you find yourself laden with feelings of guilt because you have missed a day, a week, or more, then try gathering your thoughts in a way that has more meaning for you. Instead of words, use pictures, mind maps, doodles, or a combination of some or all of these if it helps you to do it more often. There are no fixed rules of expression.

A word to the wise, however: there are many behavioral experts who recommend that focusing on changing behavior consistently, for a minimum period of 21 days, is necessary for a lasting effect. The 21-day rule is said to work because you are training your brain to think in a different way. In effect, you are sending a message via your neural pathways that shouts: "Thought diversion: this way to positivity!" So it is worth persevering.

Gratitude does not exist only in the current moment. Reviewing times of thankfulness and gratitude for past events can offer great comfort at any time, as well as helping us to adjust and broaden our perspective.

GETTING OUT OF YOUR OWN WAY

You may find yourself feeling skeptical about starting a gratitude journal. "What is the point? What a cliché. What good will it do? I haven't got time…" There are many reasons why we might tell ourselves that there is no point in giving the process a try. If you find yourself feeling resistant to the idea, perhaps pause to ask yourself: What have I got to lose?

As someone who was initially doubtful that my journal would be much more than a list of "thank yous," I was amazed at how quickly and how profoundly the process affected the way I viewed my experiences. Because the journal is intended only for positive thoughts, it forces the writer to find a way to reframe everyday happenings. The scientists are right. By deliberately choosing a positive outlook we do gradually alter the way we think—about ourselves and about the events that happen to us and around us. Expressing gratitude in a conscious way encourages us to adopt a new attitude, tweaking word choices and thought processes to open the heart and change the way we view the world.

In reality, it is impossible to hold every moment of gratitude in your memory, not even those that seem indelibly printed on your heart. Capturing passing moments in your journal is the equivalent of creating a personal album that you can look through for reinforcement and treasure forever. It frees your mind to tune in to other things, as well. It becomes self-perpetuating and takes the mind beyond itself, to the bigger picture.

REMEMBER THE 21-DAY RULE

WHY DO WE FIND IT SO HARD TO DO SIMPLE THINGS THAT ARE GOOD FOR US?

Some people who begin their gratitude journal with enthusiasm may abandon the idea before it becomes a habit. Maybe positive thoughts begin to flow more easily and it feels unnecessary to write them down; or perhaps, after a long day, it feels "too much" to spend time gathering your thoughts.

When negativity becomes the dominant state of mind, positivity becomes irritating and feels irrelevant. Grumbling can become a verbal comfort blanket that provides an illusion of control. When life is tough, anger and tiredness can get in the way of self-care. In such moments we may need to adopt a conscious change of mind to adjust our direction and chart a course back toward gratitude—one thought at a time.

GRATITUDE AT YOUR FINGERTIPS

These pages bring together thoughts and suggestions from throughout the book. They are summarized here and overleaf so that you can dip in to remind yourself of some of the ways you can re-anchor yourself. If you want to take a more intuitive approach, close your eyes and let your finger land anywhere on the page, then take on board the idea for the day!

Be appreciative. Notice any situation that leads you to appreciate what you have in your life. Where possible, think about what you can do to improve a situation for someone else.

Be thankful for the food you eat. Be mindful of the food you prepare and eat. Take time to appreciate how it smells and tastes. Focus on how healthy foods are nourishing your body and be thankful.

Be thoughtful in your gift-giving. Think about upcoming birthdays or Christmas and plan how you might change your present-giving habits. Reflect on the people you are giving to, thinking about what they bring to your life and how you can properly show your appreciation.

Give something away. Tune into your generosity and think about what you could give away? Or you could simply make a donation or give of your time.

Create a personal pot of gratitude. Fill it with ways to say thank you. This can be a real or metaphorical, depending on whether you want a physical reminder or whether contemplating it is enough to focus your thoughts.

Practice the power of 3. Note down three things to be grateful for each day this week and then reflect and expand on them.

Be grateful for differences. Appreciate differences and celebrate and be glad of diversity and all that it brings to your life.

Focus on having enough. Try to be grateful for what you have without always hungering for something seemingly bigger or better.

Pay it forward. Think about a good deed someone has done for you. How can you pay it forward?

Choose a hero. Take a moment to appreciate family, friends, neighbors, and coworkers. Honor those who contribute to your world.

Be thankful for nature. Plan a nature discovery weekend and take the time to notice and be grateful for your surroundings.

Find a gratitude challenge. Think about whether there is something you could undertake for a good cause? Is there an organization that you'd like to thank, someone you'd like to remember?

Be thankful for your skills. Have you stopped lately to think about your own unique talents and abilities and be thankful for them?

Celebrate your life. Reflect on every stage of your life so far. What were the key moments? Who were the key people? What were the most positive things that happened to you?

Be thankful for right now. By appreciating the present moment and not trying to change it, we can find greater contentment.

Make a personal gift. Call on the skills you have or learn some new skills to create something special that shows true love and thanks.

FURTHER REFLECTIONS

"LET US BE THANKFUL TO PEOPLE
WHO MAKE US HAPPY; THEY ARE THE GARDENERS
WHO MAKE US BLOSSOM."

Marcel Proust (1871–1922), writer

FURTHER REFLECTIONS

"PEOPLE MAY FORGET WHAT YOU SAID OR FORGET
WHAT YOU DID, BUT THEY WILL NEVER FORGET HOW
YOU MADE THEM FEEL."

Anonymous

CHECKLIST OF ACTIVITIES

Mark off activities as you've completed them, and perhaps make a note of ones that particularly helped you. You can then refer to this list when looking for ideas on ways to enhance your gratitude.

☐ **Week 1**   ☐ **Week 10**   ☐ **Week 19**

☐ **Week 2**   ☐ **Week 11**   ☐ **Week 20**

☐ **Week 3**   ☐ **Week 12**   ☐ **Week 21**

☐ **Week 4**   ☐ **Week 13**   ☐ **Week 22**

☐ **Week 5**   ☐ **Week 14**   ☐ **Week 23**

☐ **Week 6**   ☐ **Week 15**   ☐ **Week 24**

☐ **Week 7**   ☐ **Week 16**   ☐ **Week 25**

☐ **Week 8**   ☐ **Week 17**   ☐ **Week 26**

☐ **Week 9**   ☐ **Week 18**   ☐ **Week 27**

☐ Week 28   ☐ Week 38   ☐ Week 48

☐ Week 29   ☐ Week 39   ☐ Week 49

☐ Week 30   ☐ Week 40   ☐ Week 50

☐ Week 31   ☐ Week 41   ☐ Week 51

☐ Week 32   ☐ Week 42   ☐ Week 52

☐ Week 33   ☐ Week 43

☐ Week 34   ☐ Week 44

☐ Week 35   ☐ Week 45

☐ Week 36   ☐ Week 46

☐ Week 37   ☐ Week 47

REFERENCES

All quotations included in the book remain © copyright of the authors and are acknowledged as follows:

Page 19 S. L. Kerr, A. O'Donovan, & C. A. Pepping (2015), *Journal of Happiness Studies* 16: 17. doi:10.1007/s10902-013-9492-1

Page 63 A more complete meditation by Jack Kornfield can be found at "Meditation on Gratitude and Joy." www.jackkornfield.com/meditation-gratitude-joy

Page 72 Sara B. Algoe, Shelly L. Gable, and Natalya C. Maisel, "It's the Little Things: Everyday Gratitude as a Booster Shot for Romantic Relationships," *Personal Relationships*, 2010, available at www.sciencedaily.comreleases/2010/05/100524072912.htm. See also www.saraalgoe.com/bio

Page 100 Pilar Godino, *The Business Alchemist: A road map to authentic and inspirational leadership*, Hay House, 2013

Page 131 www.bbc.co.uk/news/uk-scotland-tayside-central-38184935; www.scotsman.com/lifestyle/interview-heinrich-steinmeyer-former-pow-1-476058

Page 153 David Steindl-Rast, "Stop. Look. Go," a video on the Gratefulness.org website: www.gratefulness.org/blog/delighted-share-new-video-stop-look-go. On the same website you will find "My Private Gratitude Journal," an easy and inspiring way to get started: www.gratefulness.org/practice

ACKNOWLEDGMENTS

My great appreciation to Cindy Richards, and the team at CICO Books for their tremendous skill and creativity—with special thanks to Rebecca Smith, who wrote additional text and created ideas and activities for weeks 10, 13, 14, 16, 27, 30, 31, and 35, and the feature on pages 112–113. Thank you, too, to those who have shared their stories, provided feedback, or have contributed in some way, including: the Burges family, the Revd Canon Andrew Haviland, Sue Hook, Bev James, Libby Jones, Karen Kain, Sue Lanson, Mary Lou Nash, Vanda "Joy" North, Audrey Paisey, the Revd Mary Ridgewell, Dr Christina Volkmann, and Pat Watson. And, of course, thank you to my wonderful family, especially my father and Richard.

FURTHER RESOURCES

From books, to videos, to websites, to ideas for evolution!

INSPIRING BOOKS AND VIDEOS

Schwartzberg, Louie, "Nature. Beauty. Gratitude." (featuring David Steindl-Rast), TED, 2011, www.ted.com/talks/louie_schwartzberg_nature_beauty_gratitude

Seligman, Martin, *Learned Optimism: How to Change Your Mind and Your Life*, Nicholas Brearley Publishing, 2018

Simon-Thomas, Emiliana R., "Compassion in the Brain," YouTube, September 25, 2013, www.youtube.com/watch?v=Ie4htPTeOvA

Soul Pancake, "An Experiment in Gratitude: The Science of Happiness," July 11, 2013, www.youtube.com/watch?v=oHv6vTKD6lg

Steindl-Rast, David, "Want to Be Happy? Be Grateful," TED, 2013, www.ted.com/talks/david_steindl_rast_want_to_be_happy_be_grateful

Trice, Laura, "Remember to Say Thank You," TED, 2008, www.ted.com/playlists/talks/laura_trice_suggests_we_all_say_thank_you

PRACTICAL RESOURCES AND WEBSITES

Exercises, questionnaires, and experiments in gratitude:

Authentic Happiness

The Penn State University website offers a range of questionnaires on gratitude, happiness, and other measures of well-being. You can take part too, by following this link: www.authentichappiness.sas.upenn.edu

Franciscan Spiritual Center, "Musings on Gratitude"

www.fscaston.org/musings-on-gratitude

The Greater Good Science Center at the University of California, Berkeley

The University of Berkeley is at the forefront of current research into gratitude and its impact on our lives. Its website is a rich source of information: www.greatergood.berkeley.edu

The Happier Human

A generous-minded soul called Amit Amin has created the Happier Human website, a collection of personal musings and extensive resources: www.happierhuman.com

The Ripple Revolution

Curt Rosengren's Ripple Revolution website offers many routes to retuning our mindset to positive. This experiment is specifically focused on gratitude and is something any of us could do to great power and effect: www.ripplerevolution.com/would-this-gratitude-experiment-make-you-happier

David Steindl-Rast

www.gratefulness.org

ACADEMIC STUDIES

Many of these resources have been referred to during research for this book.

David DeSteno, Ye Li, Leah Dickens, and Jennifer S. Lerner, "Gratitude: A Tool for Reducing Economic Impatience," *Psychological Science* 25 (April 2014), 1262–67

Robert A. Emmons and Michael E. McCullough, "Counting Blessings Versus Burdens: An Experimental Investigation of Gratitude and Subjective Well-being in Daily Life," *Journal of Personality and Social Psychology* 84/2 (2003), 377–89, www.psy. miami.edu/faculty/mmccullough/gratitude/ Emmons_McCullough_2003_JPSP.pdf

Robert A. Emmons and Michael E. McCullough, "Highlights from the Research Project on Gratitude and Thankfulness: Dimensions and Perspectives of Gratitude," Universities of California, Davis, and Miami, 2003, www.psy.miami.edu/faculty/ mmccullough/Gratitude-Related%20Stuff/ highlights_fall_2003.pdf

"The Gratitude Questionnaire Six-item Form," www.psy.miami.edu/faculty/ mmccullough/gratitude/GQ-6-scoring-interp. pdf, from Michael E. McCullough, Robert A. Emmons, and Jo-Ann Tsang, "The Grateful Disposition: A Conceptual and Empirical Topography," *Journal of Personality and Social Psychology*, 82/1 (2002), 112–27, available at www.greatergood.berkeley.edu/pdfs/ GratitudePDFs/7McCullough- GratefulDisposition.pdf

Laura E. Kurtz, and Sara B. Algoe, "Putting Laughter in Context: Shared Laughter as Behavioral Indicator of Relationship Well- being," *Personal Relationships* 22 (2015), 573–90, doi: 10.1111/pere.12095

Michael E. McCullough, Marcia B. Kimeldorf, and Adam D. Cohen, "An Adaptation for Altruism? The Social Causes, Social Effects, and Social Evolution of Gratitude," *Current Directions in Psychological Science* 17 (2008), 281–84, www.psy.miami.edu/faculty/ mmccullough/Papers/Gratitude_CDPS_2008. pdf

Emily L. Polak and Michael E. McCullough, 'Is Gratitude an Alternative to Materialism?,' *Journal of Happiness Studies* 7 (2006), 343–60, www.psy.miami.edu/faculty/mmccullough/ Papers/gratitude_materialism.pdf

Alexandra Sifferlin, "Why Being Thankful Is Good for You," *Time*, November 23, 2015, www.time.com/4124288/thanksgiving-day- 2015-thankful-gratitude

University of North Carolina at Chapel Hill, "The Little Things: Gratitude and Shared Laughter Strengthen Romantic Partnerships," *Science Daily*, February 22, 2016, www. sciencedaily.com/ releases/2016/02/160222144546.htm

INDEX